Descriptions of Zoe has been 'wild spirited', 'dedicated', 'unconventional', 'passionate', and 'well-travelled'. She has lived in a variety of different countries, and speaks French, Spanish and Italian. She began working life as an actress, singer and dancer and performed and toured an eclectic array of theatre across Britain and Europe for many years. Zoe was raised in both urban and rural Britain, and her formative years travelling lifestyle encouraged her nomadic step later in life. Zoe enjoyed teaching English as a second language in South America, and has admirably raised four children single handedly in three different countries.

She is author to many poetry books and children's stories. She is also known as Honey.

Eli Kenneth Williamson, (EKW), who showed us the strength and dynamic of a mind, unleashed through psychosis, that illness is never a point of defeat, even when stepping into unknown territory.

To Leo Jude, to Rose Shirley, and to Giselle Daniela. My children.

To the everyday the real people, who struggle themselves.

All of you struggled against the odds, and you never left my side. Thank you, I love you.

Zoe Williamson

PSYCHOSIS TOWN: ELI'S TOWN

AUSTIN MACAULEY PUBLISHERS®

LONDON * CAMBRIDGE * NEW YORK * SHARJAH

A CIP catalogue record for this title is available from the British Library.

ISBN 9781035847488 (Paperback)
ISBN 9781035847495 (ePub e-book)

www.austinmacauley.com

First Published 2024
Austin Macauley Publishers Ltd®
1 Canada Square
Canary Wharf
London
E14 5AA

To my children. Without them, we would not have made it through to the better side.

Table of Contents

"We gave the canons of our communities across our country too much rope, and they swung us from their own pitiful gallows."

—Zoe Williamson

"You have to be sure about wanting to know me because, if you do, it's a long way ahead."

—EKW

Hello!

Hello!
Is anyone there?

999, is this you…police, please?

Can you help me, please?
Hello!

I'm running!
Running!

I'm running! Can you hear me…?

I'm running… I'm out of breath!

Hello!
What yes…?
It's my son!

My son has just run out of the house.
He is 13; he has autism; he's barefoot…

He has ADHD!
He's only…

What!
Autism!

A-U-T-I-S-M!

It's a condition, a diagnosis…

Can you hear me?

A condition…look my son…he's run out of the house; he's not well.
Eli!
ELI!
E-L-I!
Is someone coming…? Please…hello…hello.

"It is going to take a very long time for all of them to understand all of me; they just don't want to."

—EKW

Prologue

I am at the crossroads.

It is a Saturday. A glacial stillness.

White blankets of snow.

No footsteps trodden into the snow.

Virgin snow they called it.

No traffic.

It has been snowing hard.

I am in the middle of the crossing, and I am looking for my son.

It has happened again.

The sky is blue. Piles of fluffy white clouds accumulated. Darker ones behind. More snow to come.

I turn to walk and lose my footing, slip over falling, onto my side. My thigh. All of my weight is on one side. I can feel bruises forming.

I'm annoyed at myself for falling, for wasting time. My son is running through the streets in the snow.

I turn to push myself up and immediately slip.

I fall again.

I crack my face on the road.

Thin, clear, deceptive ice under layers of crunchy snow.

I feel a warm trickle down the side of my face.

I'm fine.

I'm not fine. Eli is out there somewhere.

I am thinking better of getting up, and instead, I pull myself onto my hands and knees and crawl to the road edge. I am crawling on hard snow in the middle of the crossroads. We live around the corner.

No traffic. It's snowing. No cars.

It's like a Christmas card.

I can hear sirens distantly.

For us, for Eli. Turn them off…you will frighten him.

I search for the kerb, thick with snow. And pull myself onto it. And sit and listen, to the silence, the snow and the sirens.

The rest of my children are on a bus, a coach going to Manchester.

A big Buddhist youth activity. Generation Hope.

Eli is ill. Eli cannot go to Generation Hope.

Eli is running around somewhere, barefoot, in the snow. Sub-zero temperatures, and I am sitting on the kerb of some crossroads.

Deserted, a white snow scene…

My other children are a hundred miles away.

And I think I've left the front door open.

Eli is somewhere out here.

I am perched on a kerb at the crossroads.

Snow begins to fall again. The blue skies have disappeared suddenly.

Large snowflakes fall and lay thickly.

I raise my face to the fall, and the flakes fall onto my face.

It feels nice. Just a few seconds of fresh wet snow on my skin.

Not a sound, not a breeze, not a person, no cars.

Just me. Static. Not moving…frozen in memories.

I can hear sirens, though.

The unbelievable has now happened.

I think my own insanity is beginning to relieve me of responsibility.

I think of my other children on the coach.

I remember all the doctors, psychiatrists and the social workers.
How they are anchored in paperwork.

They have done nothing.
They have not turned up.
Eli is not better.
It has not gone away.

Eli has run off again. The demons keep returning to him.
I cannot relieve him of them.

Eli, where are you?
I feel chilled.
Worried Eli will contract pneumonia. Worried he will get arrested.
Again…
Or his feet would be so frozen in frostbite; they would become black and be
amputated.
All in a few seconds. Mother-worry-thoughts.
I feel warm crusting on my face.

A wind has built up and begins to bluster through the streets.
I am the only person in the world. Right now.

Eli is running through deserted streets, holding a bread knife above his head like
the Olympic torch.

I remembered the mild terror in the professional's eyes when they met my son.
After all of them edged cautiously toward the front door. All of them shuffling
about on the periphery.

I begin moving again, so many things in my head, and I am crawling along the
road. In the snow.
I lose my footing again and have flopped onto my stomach.
Too much ice.

I am spread out like an animal.
My arms spread eagled; I am a star.
Flat on the road.

I feel exhausted.

I keep slipping. I have bruised my legs now.
My face is cut.
I cannot stand up straight.
My son is delusional.
It is snowing.
No one is listening.

Drop the knife, Eli, wherever you are.
Don't make a fuss.
Put your hands up where they can see them. Lose the knife.

Don't let them find you with a knife.
It's just a knife.

I am sitting in the snow, and I am rocking.
Eli rocks.
He says it keeps him safe. He feels safe.

I am sitting, rocking in my own personal frozen madness.

I'm grieving the system.
I'm grieving my son, my children and the snow.

I don't even hear the soft motor engine rumble nearby as it pulls up.
Voices.

Doors opening and shutting.

"Zoe?"
"Are you Zoe, love?"

Warmth wraps me up. and strong arms pull me to my feet and the body next to me and manoeuvre me into a car, a police car.

Eli is sitting behind.

He has a puffy jacket on. It's not his; he doesn't wear puffy jackets.

He looks worried about me.

The madness has lifted.

"You're bleeding, Mum!"

Eli's voice. Eli sounds worried, alarmed and back to normal.

"Stay there, son; she's alright... Let's get you in the car, love... Don't worry she's fine. ...You're Eli's mum, right? Let's get you home..."

"Where we are now, is not who we are meant to be."

—EKW

Part One
Eli

I have four children.

My son, Eli, was diagnosed with ASD and ADHD when he was five and a half years old.

We had returned to the UK a few months before.
He is the third-born out of my four children.

When my son Eli turned 13, he experienced a mental health breakdown.
He crashed emotionally.
It was summer 2017.
He was swallowed by a dark, all-consuming living nightmare.

Nothing prepared us for it.
He descended very quickly.

I called out for help.
No help came.
So I called for help again.

Something that would restore life to normality.
Something to give us hope.
Then we waited.
And we kept waiting.

Take Him to A&E...

We took Eli to the main city hospital A&E because he had fallen ill and was very unwell.

This was the continuous suggestion of the professionals we called out to. So we did it.

He had become distressingly out of control.

Police had arranged an ambulance. Here at home.

Police were the only ones to take notice.

After hours waiting in A&E, Eli became rapidly worse.

His younger brother was with me.

Eli was removed from me to another area of the hospital as patients complained about him threatening me; it was agreed he stay in the hospital in the children's ward until a location could be found to suit his needs.

A member of the CAMHS team had come to assess him.

Social services had suggested he stay with a friend.

It was 2:00 am.

When what I had thought the formations of a nightmare were emerging, were just tipping the iceberg.

I had no idea what was in store for any of us.

Eli continued to fall apart throughout the night and early morning.

Social services did not arrive.

We arrived at 6:30 that evening and left the hospital the next morning at 5:35.

The CAMHS advisor had even listened to my younger son who was 12, Eli's younger brother.

He was Eli's young carer.

She was advised by her senior to come in and evaluate Eli; she did and concluded he needed help.

I was led to believe a tier 4 bed.

He would stay in the hospital until a suitable place could be located.

A bed was found for Eli in the children's ward, meantime, to be assessed later on by the psychiatrist.

There was no support in place for his autism or extreme aggressive behaviour although this had been explained and witnessed over and over again.

Meantime, CTR next day and psychiatrist.

Children's ward meant to keep him safe could not cope with him.

My youngest son was now asleep on one of the trolleys.

This hospital is an hour and a half on the bus.

There was no public transport at this time in the morning.

I had had no sleep at all.

I was asked by the ward nurse what time I would be arriving back at the hospital in the morning.

Bearing in mind we had no idea how to return home and then come back to the hospital.

"You have to be here when CAMHS come in." She looked up from her notes.

"CAMHS have already been in," I said. She rummaged through her notes.

The hospital sent us home in a taxi where we promptly fell into bed.

Eli was becoming enraged. He did not want to see me.

This was interpreted as a parenting thing. Resulting from his decline in mental health.

The next day, an emergency CTR occurred… They kept talking about scandals at residential hospitals and how they had to be careful.

What resulted was a location being required to suit Eli's needs.

I was also taking calls from the children's ward.

Eli had become completely out of control on the ward.

There was no one to deal with his autism or his mental health issues.

I was at home and could not get back to hospital.

I had no car.

It was miles away.

The bus took an hour and a half.

The train took two hours, and I needed two trains.

I was expected to appear in the next five minutes with medication, clothes, food, money for him and a calming presence.

I still had Eli's siblings at home.

Emergency CTR was to find a suitable placement for him.

After two days on the children's ward staff called the police.

Eli was arrested.

No one was interested in his deteriorating health at this point.

He was very unwell, and just 13, no one could cope with him. And no one had enlightened knowledge about autism.

They were trying to reason with him.

The police were only interested in the criminality.

The psychiatrist deemed him well and fit.

She was extremely sarcastic to me because I stressed to her she was not listening.

I realised that she was not going to do anything productive for my son's declining state of mind.

She repeated my last line of dialogue back to me as evidence and said, "You see I am listening to you."

Eli was arrested by the police.

The children's ward called the police because they could not contain him although they had originally said they would take care of him.

He was handcuffed, read his rights and marched out of the hospital by the police.

Eli was 13 he was amidst a serious mental health breakdown; he was totally psychotic; and he was arrested from the hospital meant to be keeping him safe.
He already had ASD and ADHD diagnosed disorders.
This was something else.
Something very different.

Then he remained in police custody all night.

They would not listen to me about his learning disabilities.
I was at home, without a car. It was late at night.
I received a call from the hospital to tell me what they had done.
Eli was in miles away in police custody.

I received a call from the police detention centre over 30 miles away in the morning who wanted to know if I wanted Eli back home.
The officer would not listen to anything I had to say; he was interested only in the criminality.

The next morning, the police detention officers tried to make Eli read legal details he did not understand, and he was expected to have an interview with a solicitor.
He couldn't; he kept falling apart.

This did not stop the police from photographing him and taking his fingerprints.
My son was now a criminal in their eyes.
And they were not listening to me.
Their composure gave me the impression they had no interest in listening to me.

This situation within custody detention would put the most intelligent, able-bodied and able-minded ill at ease.

This is the regular go-to for the services.

If your child has become out of control, call the police.
And this is what the hospital did.
They could not cope; they called the police.

We were asked about a social worker or key worker.

But Eli still had no professionals supporting us.

There was no social worker or CAMHS assessment/input.

I had hoped that some degree of success would have been achieved during this stay in the hospital.

Instead, it turned into something despairing, dissolute.

It had been a nightmare.

Very little attention was given to Eli's disorientation or his mental health deterioration.

I tried to explain about his learning disabilities, his ASD, etc. His inability to read for his age group.

They had tried to make him read legal legislation.

He couldn't.

So I read it.

I did try and impress he could not read very much and not in a concentrated way.

Sentences needed to be broken down; otherwise, he would get angry.

He has ADHD.

One of the officers said to me that it sounded as if I had a little bit of ADHD myself.

Eli kept falling apart in police custody.

Reduced to incoherent babble.

Foaming and crying when he did not correspond as the officers might have liked he was bent over in the arm clasp to restrain him.

I watched as my son, now helpless in the hands of detention officers, was manhandled around the centre.

They were not listening to me.

They put his hands behind his back, and he could not stand up straight.

He was crying and blaspheming.

I was unsure how much I could say before being arrested myself.

Or how to control myself.
Eli was getting worse, and they were trying to reason with him.

So I stood by helpless.
This was the professional's answer to all things, and it still is.
Take him to A&E. Call the police.

Eyebrows raised when they learned there was no social worker, almost as if it were my fault.

I felt dirty, and I felt unheard. I felt like a nuisance and a hindrance and that my son should just be wiped from the map.
The mother of a thug.
One officer told me, "Well, they are all ADHD, aren't they, at this point love?"

And another told me to try and read books about autism.

I don't know what happened to make the officers do what they did next, but they dropped all charges, and we could go.

We had been trying to find help for Eli.
My son had crashed into unfathomable depths.
He was unrecognisable.
We followed advice from CAMHS who were still not engaging, offering appointments or agreeing Eli should even be seen by them. He purportedly did not meet their criteria.

We followed the advice of social services who were equally not engaged.

He had been placed on a ward to get further help, but help did not arrive and those on the ward had little understanding or support for autism.
So that was it.
That was A&E.

A&E is the place to receive medical help.
Eli received an arrest.

***

On another occasion, Eli had self-harmed, and I had managed to get him to A&E.

I was informed by the A&E nurse that she wouldn't let her children self-harm.

Eli was deemed fit and well by mental health authorities and a 'care package' would be supplied.

We were reluctant to use A&E again.
When police were called, they hung about like voracious vultures, hands-on handcuffs, eager to manacle Eli.

Eli was nothing more than a recalcitrant boy.
And there was no social worker.

Take him to A&E.
That is what we did, and it resulted in Eli being arrested.

After the entire event, no one came by to check on us or see how things were.

"My name is Eli and you will never understand it all, I get scared of my own mind and do they think they can understand that."

—EKW

First Encounter with Social Services

I was offered a foster home by social services for Eli.

They believed I did not want Eli.

I do not understand how a foster family would have made things better.

Paediatrician

Community paediatrics diagnosed Eli with ASD and ADHD.

No one diagnosed him with learning disabilities.

Paediatrics prepared me for what was to come, the journey ahead through autism and ADHD and that mental health complications could override, but more so, by the difficulties that we could face as families.

We were pre-warned by paediatrics of the struggle that would ensue in the community and in our own lives and through social activity and society in general.

Perhaps most of all those professionals at all levels, and all in all places, would let us down and not hear us, close the doors wherever possible, putting their fingers in their ears.

(If they can't hear us then it isn't happening)

The Social Services

The social services are a section of local government authority, in charge of a providing assistance and care for vulnerable children and adults, and families.
About focusing on what is needed to make a better, improved life all around.
To promote the well-being of the child and adult in need.
That is what should be happening.
That is what I had hoped would happen.

A Five-Minute Worker

The first line of the very first social service reports stated that I did not want Eli in the house anymore.

This was the introduction of their service into our lives and for us into their state of things.

We were, in fact, a family in chaos.
The social service report stated that Eli's behaviour was because we were in chaos.

It suggested 'Mum' should take parenting classes.

I had been parenting four children, on my own, for over 25 years at this point.

Referrals and Walking into Walls

We have gone to the GP and the paediatrician.

We keep going back.

Every time Eli runs off into the streets, every time Eli pulls apart my home, throwing furniture down the stairs, overturning tables and sofas.

He is very strong.

Every time he opens the windows and shouts out, he is not safe, and they are coming for him and 'Help me!' each time we return.

A different GP each time.

Some listen; others yawn.

Some look at their watches and check phones, and others tell us we already have CAMHS in place because CAMHS have appeared on their notes.

So take it up with them.

The paediatrician is worried.

She has never seen him like this before.

She normally sees him every six months.

We have all built up a strong relationship. Eli likes talking with her, and she and I have a good communicative relationship.

We talk about many things, all kinds of worldly things, and Eli talks about his dreams, and she listens and agrees and smiles. She is very lovely.

She talks about her patients as her children.

She loves them.

She now sees Eli every week.

She has referred him again.

She has become really concerned.

She is trying, and she is concerned; she is really concerned about this demise, such a decline in his behaviour.

She tells me that he is experiencing a mental health breakdown.

She calls it a CRASH.

She also pre-warns me how difficult it will be to get anyone to listen to me.

She wonders whether a different ADHD medication might help.

She prescribes something that works very differently from what he usually takes.

Sometimes, the medication counteracts the hyperactivity of ADHD helping to create a consistency in the brain, allowing better focus.

This new medicine works slowly and must be monitored through weight and blood pressure so that the dosage can be built up gently. This will prevent any form of collapse or fainting.

But it is taking too long to take effect.

We do not want Eli to pass out.

So we change the medication back.

On top of Eli's breakdown, he is now more than hyperactive because he is totally undermedicated for his ADHD.

Life has thrown us all into the pitfalls of some underworld hell.

I cannot control Eli.

The GPs (community doctors) have referred him to mental health services.

Several times now.

CAMHS.

Nothing happens. I call CAMHS, but they need a referral from the GP.

I call the GP.

I burst into tears with the doctor's surgery receptionist.

She is so understanding. She has a child with ASD and ADHD.

She knows this journey.

She is being nice.

It is the heart of the summer holidays.

No school.

The paediatrician decides after three weeks to stop this new medication and revert to the old one.

We do, and at least Eli's ADHD is medicated as it was before the old medication.

Nothing stops his violence.

He has begun hitting me.
And his brother.

Where are the services?

Care Packages and Crisis Plans

Care plans and packages and all the other terms, are procedural.
They are put in place for me.
To tell me what to do with my son, who I live with.

These had been put in place by people who did not know us.

These plans and packages are pulled out of a system.
They have been fortified by people who spend 20 minutes a week in my house with Eli.

"I can't control it. Mum…it comes over me…then it leaves me, so I didn't have any choices… I am not prepared or ready for anything… I want to stop the violence."

—EKW

The Snake Uncoils, and Venom Drips

Eli had pulled apart my house so much that I had begun removing items and locking things away.

We moved the upright piano into a neighbour's house.

And musical instruments into the loft and to my eldest daughter's house.

Eli had become so violent and aggressively tried to upsurge his life into some sort of meaning.

My fear that police would arrive, arrest him, and his route forward would become criminal came true.

This would not help him.

Nothing was helping him.

We awoke each day into a brand-new fresh hell.

Police officers have told me to read books on autism.

And had little understanding of autism themselves.

Mental health in young people is a continuous nightmare…against raging hormones, and battling emotions, darkness descends into crashing, silent clouds, thick and dense, covering everything that makes sense. It is a continuous horror that one cannot wake up from…

Children always turn to their point of safety when the world has become too much.

Sometimes, it is the parents. Mother. So he turns to me. It's Me.

Then he turns on me.

But it is OK he is ill.

Safety releases their feelings, emotions, self-beliefs, their corrupted esteem and self-doubt.

On top of all of Eli's daily demands, the extreme challenges he went through, the extraneous global perceptions, what he believed the world to be and how it actually was, what he expected, the reality of his limited academic ability, his lack of focus, his need to have support at all times, his nuances and oddities and routines all began to dissemble, as he started to disintegrate emotionally, and his mental stability fell to rock bottom.

The person he had become was a shadow of the boy he once was.

He had no idea where his world began or ended, or where the sense was to anything. We had coped forever with his sensory meltdowns and fixations…his obsessive behaviours and dislike of things, avoiding pictures and animated faces, preparing food in certain ways…just knowing his ways…but what happened during this breakdown in 2017 we could never have been prepared for. What were once his routines were now distant memories and had no place in his now-fettered, chattering, crazed world.

Of voices and noises that none of us could hear.

Of unfamiliar, frightening sounds.

Finding no relief…tears of hopeless agony, beating his head against the doors.

Arriving at my side with blood staining his face, trickling down the sides of his face, not letting me clean him, gripping with a monster clench my wrists, a fearful, desperation in his eyes and staring vacantly into mine, life had disappeared from his world and did not shine from him anymore.

Eli would sit with me whilst I did some yoga or chanted, or cooked dinner, his eyes glazed, a madness pummelling in his head, a madness he could not control. And all of this I had to transpose and find a way for CAMHS to acknowledge what was happening.

***

Eli has taken to running into the road and lying down, inviting cars to run over him.

He jumps onto car rooftops and bounces across them.

He screams intelligibly into the night, from the garden.
He has crawled up the drainpipe and almost took it off the wall.

Sometimes in the daytime, neighbours take out deckchairs and put them in their front gardens to watch.

Others rev up their motorbikes and cars and help us chase after Eli as he makes another attempt to escape the demons and goes charging off into the streets.

WHERE ARE THE SERVICES?

First Meeting with CAMHS

When CAMHS finally met Eli, it was 14 September 2017.

We had called out countless times and pleaded with doctors and the paediatrician who saw the decline in Eli so desperately themselves and referred him.

We were offered an appointment with CAMHS months into the new year, and then that was moved back further back.

Eli was now unintelligible.

Eli was very very ill; after using what I had left which were drops of my own self-preservation, for some great time, for movement forward, a date appeared for Eli to meet CAMHS.

14 September 2017.

We will never forget this day.

And so, we went.

This date had been pushed back originally, into November and December of 2017.

Suddenly a date became available the next week, we took it!

First, we met with the crisis team who suggested Eli meet the core team because he was not a crisis.

He was pulling apart his home and destroying the contents of his home, running, off, jumping onto car rooftops, getting arrested, screaming out unintelligibly, and assaulting his family members.

Calling the police himself begging them to take him away from the burning hell that was consuming him.

Calling random numbers asking them to do the same.

However, he was not standing on a bridge threatening to jump off, trying to drown himself in a bath or taking pills to stop breathing, or throwing himself from a window.

Or stabbing himself, shooting himself or anyone else.

He was in fact still alive, dressed (sometimes not) and talking.

He was not dead.

Therefore, this was not a crisis.

He did not 'present' as if he was in crisis.

There was no purported suicidal ideation.

He was not depressed or in a 'low mood'.

He looked as if he had eaten something.

We were offered a date for the core team.

It took a while to get Eli together, some persuasion, and after convincing him that at some point his dreams would become accomplished, he would meet band members, and wear a fur suit, and everything was pushed aside for this precious date.

Finally, Eli was ready, prepared, and quite calm and off we went.

He met the disability nurse who would remain indirectly throughout the process until residential school.

He became fixated with her.

And this, she used to her advantage in the months to come.

Whilst this fixation was a contributor of autism.

He just fixated on her.

Autism can fixate on people and things.

And situations.

She began to indirectly at first, persuade her notes that she was 'working' with him.

There was another person with the nurse.

I can only presume she was a psychologist. I don't know because they did not introduce themselves and did not warm up the meeting by chatting with us. It was clinical and official and the assessment began.

We were sitting in the waiting room, we were beckoned into a room.

They began shuffling papers around.

Eli just wanted to talk about his issues and how he was feeling.

They launched straight into the assessment.

Papers, ticking boxes, pencils, clicking pens... I had one to fill out too... Eli became exhausted after about 30 minutes.

They were going to stop and do some more another time, and we were about to leave when Eli ran out into the waiting room and began kicking the main doors. With some horror from staff, he was pursued by the CAMHS nurse and psychologist who tried to allay him and asked him to not kick the doors.

"Please, Eli," one said. "There are children here."

And they managed to bring him back into the room where they had begun and asked me to sit outside.

I went into a special little waiting room for CAMHS patients.

There was no one else there.

I could hear Eli.

Through two sets of double doors.

He was crying out and screaming.

An alarm went off, I thought was the fire alarm, but in fact, it alerted other staff members to come rushing into the vicinity where Eli was.

Furniture was being removed from the room; I tried to go in to see what was happening.

Eli saw me and snarled, "Get her away from me!" And I had to leave again.

This continued...calling out, thuds, objects being thrown and hurled, furniture removed...alarms going off, staff running to the assembled room...he never left the room.

And no one communicated with me. I was remotely hopeful that this was indicative of how he was in real life. Something was wrong, clearly wrong.

This would be the catalyst for future development.

My children at home, one who had been discharged from hospital the day before and Eli's youngest brother, came running down the road to be with me.

A member of staff brought us all to another area of the mental health hub.

She saw we were hungry and called out for biscuits. And squash.

(I learned later that the learning disability nurse had referred to this as us being 'managed' by staff).

Eli continued to progressively get worse. The locum psychiatrist was called and went in to see him.

By the time she saw me, I was at my wit's end.

It was nearing 2:00 pm. I had not eaten.

The rest of my family were still in the hub now.

My eldest daughter had an appointment there and stayed to offer support.

We were all there.

Eli had not eaten. We had been there for five hours.

No one spoke to us at all. I had to keep going to the room Eli was in.

Terrified every time the alarm went off, and staff came surging forth that police would be called.

I was hysterical.

I cried my heart out to friends and family members for some support, reassurance or something on my phone.

Make it stop. Make it better.

Everyone was hoping that now Eli was within the surroundings of the mental health hub they would finally realise he was ill and get him deserved help.

The doctor agreed he needed help but because he wanted to go to the hospital she could not section him. They were looking for a hospital.

A tier 4 hospital.

One had been found.

They just needed transport.

I was even spoken to by the financial side of the CAMHS department to get transport allocated.

My youngest son ran home to pack clothes and gadgets for Eli, and to bring back his ADHD medication.

Methylphenidate.

Eli had fallen asleep on the floor.

He was in the same room, on the floor, asleep, exhausted.

It was about 4:00 pm. Other patients had had their appointments cancelled.

Still, he had not eaten. No food had been brought in to him apart from a packet of crisps.

The waiting room was on red alert, it was darkened and doors locked.

Eli throughout his ten hours was offered nothing to eat.

His brother ran home and made sandwiches for him and brought them back in, along with clothes and devices, because we had been led to believe Eli would be going into hospital.
But they did not allow him in to give the sandwiches.

The learning disability nurse was quoted in a social report by the social services that I had been 'playing the victim'.

The day when I had hoped peace might arrive and some sustainable amount of normality assumed.
Help from a body of professionals calling themselves mental health services.
A level of understanding and sympathy for what Eli was struggling with.
A duty from them to us, to Eli, to his mental health.
I had believed the beginning of something magnificent.

Violence Resumed

Eli had arisen from his sleep. Hungry and unnerved, nothing had resulted from any of this. He was on the CAMHS therapy room floor, and after some calm, resumed his despair.

Nothing was happening.

Eli tore apart the CAMHS therapy room.

They had not moved him.

He had not ventured out of the room.

Nothing to eat.

I couldn't go in to see him.

We seemed to be waiting now for transport to the hospital only in the next community city.

A bed had been secured. But nothing else happened.

Time carried on, the lights went out and the doors closed.

The public and staff members went home.

I saw a member of staff shrug her shoulders at reception at some shocking news, shaking her head...she disappeared into the corridor where Eli was.

At 7:30 pm, the nurse and psychologist and an unhinged Eli appeared and explained that the whole hospital thing had been overruled.

There was nothing more to be done Eli had to go home.

I was taken to a small therapy room by the psychiatrist who explained she was feeling quite drained.

My youngest son remembered how the disability nurse said she would call or come over the next day.

He still recalls her saying that, even now. Years later.

And she never called or came over.

No one followed up.

Nothing else happened.

And we went home.

***

We called a taxi and went home. With Eli.

All of us. A car full of family.

Once home Eli ran off again into the night.

We, myself and my children, pursued him and brought him home.

Eventually, he began to slow down, exhausted and fell asleep. He took bio-melatonin and slept into the depths of night.

A whole bone-weary day, waiting, hoping, listening, crying…this was it now, this was the place to make him better, it was finally going to begin…

Instead we had been sent home.

The next morning, no one called us, so I called through to CAMHS.

No one was available. I gave my number and explained about yesterday.

Nothing happened, no one called back, and it remained that way.

No one else followed up with a call to see how Eli was.

No one seemed to know anything about the 10 hours that happened the day before.

I even explained that other people were having their appointments cancelled because of the madness that was going on.

A few days later, the locum psychiatrist called me and told me I shouldn't give in to Eli's wants.

I had no idea why she would say this to me.

She then asked me what I thought happened in terms of Eli not going into the hospital.

I had no idea and was unsure why she thought I would have a presumption.

Then she suggested he go on Risperidone.

A medication to help alleviate some of the violence.

She saw him a couple of months later and made note that he was well-presented and not showing any signs of deterioration.

***

When you turn up to your appointment with the mental health services and look clean and well-presented, the fact that you are dressed even and have turned up, indicates to them, you are no longer in need of their services.
You are well.

You do not use terms like depressed, these are known as low mood.

You may be offered charts from 0 to 10 about how you are feeling.

However, your answers can be changed or disagreed with, even though these answers are responses to questions about your feelings.
And one cannot repeat the same number on the graph.

If you do not turn up to your appointment, because you are unwell, they discharge you for not turning up.

If you are not threatening suicide, or self-harm you are not in need of the crisis team.
If you are feeling like you want to end your life and do not turn up to the appointment, they discharge you.

There are very long waiting lists.

If Eli is so badly ill, he has thrust his head against a wall, and I am trying to manage the rest of my family and cannot even manage to make a phone call, his residency with CAMHS is discharged. Sometimes we, the family cannot make the call quick enough, and even then when we do, we must behave in an 'acceptable' way otherwise the call will be terminated.
We must not behave as if the entire family is in crisis.
Even when, we are a family in crisis.

I am a carer, and I am a mother.

I try and maintain calm in the murky, mud-filled waters my family have now become immersed in; our lives are beyond natural conception.

Where we once lived is a peaceful, harmonious place we no longer know.

We now live in hell.

We live in Eli's nightmares.

We reside in his ephialtes-ridden purgatory.

And services that are supposed to be the tenets of society in place to assist us, do not lift a finger to help us.

Protocol has become more important than the actual needs of the young person.

We are the Family

We see what the professionals cannot.
We do what they cannot.
We are, what they are not.

The senseless and the bizarre are not strangers to my life.
They are not strangers to any carer's life.
Our efforts are inexhaustive, they have to be.

A family dedicated, together, unites amidst confusion and chaos.
And creates a solution.

We are criticised and repudiated, we are fought against, ignored, or scrutinised.

So, we start to close ranks.
And we remain on guard all the time to everything else around us.

Another Social Worker

The social worker appeared late in August 2017.
She stayed four hours in our house.
And wrote pages of notes.
She met Eli, but she did not know Eli.
She did not know he was ill.
She could not acknowledge he had worn the same clothes since the week before.
And he was smelling.
She did not know Eli, and she did not know us.

I held out hope she would give us assistance.

His eyes were glazed.
She spoke of positive futures, early help workers and parenting classes.

His eyes were glazed.
He spoke unintelligible things to her.
She noted it all.
She even asked him to spell things.
She wrote pages of notes.
She left, and we did not see her again.

She had gone.
At this point, hope was fading fast for Eli.

It was summer 2017.
No one came back.

Eli descended into darkness again.

"I didn't have any choices…"

—EKW

We are grieving the system.

Disbelief in the system that has ignored us.

Grieving because they don't care.

How do we get anyone to listen who isn't interested?

We are alone and Eli is getting worse.

He screams out for help and lies across the floor salivating.

He throws himself into walls. Then he throws himself into us.

CAMHS have still not offered any appointments or sessions but the learning disability nurse turns up for all the Child in Need meetings.

These are currently held in my home because I cannot leave Eli.

And there is no one else to take care of him.

None of this seems to register with the professionals.

Whilst the meetings go ahead, Eli is in his room, listening to his music.

Just freshly medicated with ADHD methylphenidate.

And a little lorazepam.

That has been offered.

And now Risperidone.

But nothing is being done to examine the reasons behind his decline.

Whatever is eating away at my son's soul, is not going to disappear.

The professionals all gather and talk about nonsense that is ineffectual and has nothing to do with anything about Eli.

They skim the surface.

Skip about on the periphery and ignore anything about his state of mind.

They are not listening, and they don't understand, but I let them think they do. "What else can I do, they don't get it, Mum!"

—EKW

Police Arrests

There has to be an appropriate adult with the child. Not the person who has allegedly made the call or complaint.

And in the flurry of fury and madness, Eli was caught up in his delusional, fully crazed world. The nightmare descending about cloaked in darkness made no sense to him, and we became figures and cameos of his past.

We were nothing to him in the moment of resurrected insanity, psychotic interludes, violent, and frightening.

Children spit.

Autism spits.

Mental health decline spits.

Angry people spit.

Delusion spits.

Autism spits.

Eli was arrested for spitting at an officer.

Spitting is a form of expelling something inside.

They are trying to make a statement in a way they cannot speak.

Eli was arrested in the city hospital in the children's ward.

A place that had meant to keep him safe.

The next time was for damage to property.

In school.

Pulling paper off walls.

Both times in custody Eli was interviewed by a psychiatrist. Both times he was deemed fit and well.

He did not portray any signs of mental health decline, and it was deemed his autism.

Eli was interviewed by the mental health team at midnight in police custody.

Another care package was suggested.

All these packages.

Lots of packages.

And words.

One police officer told me Eli would grow out of it.

Another did not know the difference between an early help worker and a CAMHS worker.

Another directed all of his conversation to my chest.

Others tried to reason with him.

Most had no interest in him and appeared as if they just wanted to get on with other things in their life.

A majority of officers had no idea what autism was.

It appeared the best way to deal with Eli's psychotic episodes was to arrest him, or at least handcuff him.

Lasting emotional damage.

For Eli.

For us.

No one is listening.

Eli is placed at a great disadvantage.

The first 10-hour introduction CAMHS had with Eli has just disappeared.

When the child is arrested, so is the family.

We are all tarred and brandished and bundled together.

We are all criminals.

And no one seems bothered.

In the meetings, professionals all gather together and make competent-sounding noise, and then disappear and do nothing else.

There is no sympathy, a thirteen-year-old boy with autism and ADHD who is psychotically out of control has been handcuffed and locked up.

Eli nods and says yes. Those around him who do not know him, believe he understands, and he is in control.
CAMHS have said Eli is in control and knows what he is doing.

Trauma sets in early.
The autistic brain and the ADHD brain are wired up differently.

What I am expecting from professionals is not happening.
What they publicise and promise is not happening.
What they write is spurious and affected.

Police are arresting Eli.
Eli has now been manhandled into police cars and vans.
Police officer's reaction implied that my son was attention-seeking.

> "Putting people like me in jail is just not going to work because there is still going to be more of us.
> More will come.
> They will have to listen then, won't they."

—EKW

Our journey was beyond trepidation.
We were being marched into hell.

"You see I have to make it happen, it is in my head I do not know how to get it
out."

—EKW

Another Social Worker

We had been without a social worker for approximately three months.
The next social worker appeared late in December 2017.
She had no idea who Eli was and demanded she had the diagnosis letter from the paediatrician about his diagnosis.
I did not give it to her.

I told her she was not involved because of his diagnosis.
She smelled strongly of very stale tobacco.

She told me that autism and ADHD were on the same spectrum. She knew this because she had been on a course.
According to her, they were the same thing.

And after making paper planes with Eli she stood in front of me with a serious look on her face and said her deductions were that Eli had Aspergers.
I told them I did not need to know her opinion and that he already had a diagnosis from a consultant paediatrician.

She told me she 'needed' that paperwork.
I told her this was not why she was here. However, she then added her 'prognosis' into her reports saying Eli had been diagnosed with 'mild autism'.

She held a CIN meeting where other professionals attended.
The safeguarding officers from school and CAMHS.

She observed me with a pile of Eli's new clothes on my lap.
I was unstitching labels.
She asked me what I was doing.

I replied, "This is autism."

***

This social worker put up her flip-top notebook and began tapping out information. She then asked, "What's Eli actually diagnosed with?"
I replied, "ASD and…"
"So not autism then!" she interrupted and tapped away.
There were a few gasps and astonished faces and looks of utter disbelief from everyone around the table.
Unaware she looked up and then became self-conscious.
"What!" she said and laughed nervously, "What have I said?"
I corrected her, "ASD! Autism spectrum disorder!"

She laughed embarrassed, "Oh, yes, I forgot… I forgot," and tapped away.

Her notes did not change and within a few days of the new year of 2018, she left. Her hastily put-together notes remained for some time in logged reports, much longer.

Mild autism.

This is not a permissible diagnosis from any consultant with any ounce of professionalism, it does not exist, autism is autism. It exists across a large and convoluted spectrum and is a lifelong condition.
Overlaps with other conditions, diagnosed or not.
All spectrums.
All of the chosen usual, normal grid.

Eli continued to fall into a deep, darkening hell.
It wouldn't be too long before we followed after him.

Educational Psychologist

We met her on a cold and bitter January morning.
The early help worker drove us.

I am unsure what the achieved goal was meant to be.
The social worker who put the educational psychology in place was gone.

The educational psychologist kept showing Eli a clock telling him she did not have much time left.

Eli cannot conceptualise time.
He worries we are always running out of time.
The clock and the ed psych were not helpful, we had no idea what it was meant to be about.

And my son fell into another abyss of descending darkness.

The Ephialtes

From quiet emerged disruption, chaos…demons of wild and unleashed devils spawn…my house barely contained anything and Eli had destroyed everything else.

Violence had become part of the walls. The floor. The roof.

Our lives and despair now were the oxygen we breathed.

The thudding, the kicking walls.

The opening and closing and slamming of windows.

The plates smashed the screaming, the moaning, the desperation.

Shaking me.

Get him someone to make it go away.

It was all becoming part of a demented reality.

Ourselves getting vexed about which way was normal.

And which way was out.

Because we could not find the way in.

Every day another point of survival until Eli, finally exhausted fell into a deep, dreamless sleep, and I could piece together what fragments remained.

And hope.

There was always hope.

I often had to search for it and had no idea where hope might be, but it had to be there.

***

"Are they coming to get me now, have they found somewhere."

—EKW

There is no social worker.

No CAMHS workers.

The last social worker left in the early days of January 2018.

There were still no appointments, sessions, or therapy from CAMHS or any social workers.

The early help workers were at a stage of bewilderment.

"I am not ready or prepared."

—EKW

Support

Professionals insisted they were supporting us.
They logged phone calls and meetings and wrote down any conversations and emails sent. That was it.

Because of their own failings, things were a mess.
They refused Eli because of his autism and his ADHD.

In all correspondence, uniformed rhetoric is used.
Basically, it sounds good but is totally ineffective.

Notes leaving the hands of predecessor going into successor is much like passing a handful of water into another pair of hands.
Water is going to fall out, drip out.

This is what happens with notes.

It's like a game of Chinese whispers.
Notes are missed out and messy; the chronology is not accurate and rewritten; and the narrative often suits the author.

What this all began as is something quite different now.

Vesanus

Eli continued to deteriorate and tore apart the house. He pulled up rugs, tore up carpets, and pulled over a heavy bookcase, full of books ornaments trinkets.

He upturned armchairs and sofas and ran outside to jump across people's cars.

He lay in the road.

He smashed dishes and pressed his face against the windows as if trying to 'get out', his sweat and saliva smudged into the windowpanes.

He drew his own blood from anything he could make sharp. Paper cuts. Pencils, his own nails.

His body fluids dripped around our house.

He smeared his blood across the walls inside the house.

He laughed frantically in the garden and thrashed himself into trees.

Eli is very strong.

Unlimited strength to upturn furniture, heavy, weighted objects on their sides or upturned, and sometimes rendered useless.

He cried out relentlessly and beat his head against walls and doors.

He pulled off his shoes and clothes and threw them.

He broke a massive mirror in our house, and we can still find shards lodged into corners of the floor.

Eventually, his violence progressed into the outside, the hills that were behind my house, and he would disappear.

Racing about in frenetic, wild movements.

Laughing wildly and crying out at the top of his voice.

Police called through and told me to keep an eye on things.

And, still, no one came to our rescue.

Advice across the phone lines went as follows:

Store away Disinfectant, scourers, nail files, broken eggshells, and the forks. Maybe the spoons too.

All the 'sharps'. Anything like dinner knives, bread knives, chopping knives, scissors, compasses, nailfiles, the list was endless.

Some told me it would take an hour to cross town through the traffic, so they could not do that.

Other times they just refused to come out or did not answer.

This was the extent of the crisis interaction.

I had to dismantle the landline, as Eli was tapping in random numbers and discussing his problems with whoever answered.

And he kept calling 999 asking for an ambulance and police to come and tie me up because I was failing to get the right people to help him.

Eli broke fixtures ripped out plants, and broke apart garden furniture.

He cried and shouted to 'get it all out' of him. And, sometimes, he would sink into the depths of darkness like I had never seen.

On his bed motionless, staring in a strange state of catatonic trance, unable to respond.

Tears of magnitude well in his eyes.

He beat his head with his knuckles and cried wearily, "They won't go away. Make it go away, Mum!"

There were times he was so angry, his eyes fierce with rage and confusion he tore into the walls to find anything to cut himself.

We can only reduce the possibility of self-harm.

Eli would carve into his arms like carving a roast.

I would bind his arms after he was relieved of his hours of madness with moments of sanity.

There were times he secretly dug his nails into old wounds to reopen them and watched the blood come to the surface and trickle through.

Violence progressed onwards, and Eli began to lunge towards me and my younger son.

We spent hours in anguish every day dodging the ever-incrementing challenges from Eli's breakdown.

And no one came by, no one called through, no one answered my calls, my cries for help.

No one heard us.

"When are they coming for me, Mum?" Eli called out to me.

"Call CAMHS!"

I called every possible outlet I could think of, independent services and agencies that charged a lot of money to give advice about 'coping' with Eli.

No one could give bespoke advice.

Eli fell into an endless hole of darkness turning blacker and more profound.

Something was wrong, badly, insanely wrong.

His world of dreams and Minecraft, and music flooding through his ears was gone.
He began to razor his arms and legs and his forehead.

I spoke to a co Ordinator in CAMHS who told me he is not self-harming any more.

Who is going to follow Eli and us into the bottomless well of psychotic nightmare?

Where were they?

Where are the canons of society?
Where are the services?

"If you become me then you can't sleep because if I think about it all, you feel so little."

—EKW

In the World According to Eli

"There are all the moons and planets and the gods and magic, and it is much
bigger than all of that, and it grows and travels on and becomes a different
world. Magic places become portals and open up, and we can dive in and go
somewhere else, but it scares me because you all want to be like me but you
have to get very small to be like me.
You wouldn't like it because of its hard work."

—EKW

***

"Are they just covering their ears?"

—EKW

No professional would hear us and no one would listen. We had reached out to every outlet, to every corner of society, all medical relief, every social service, all the while unable to calm my family home, as I watched with terror my son become worse, and my family deconstruct.

Madness was here.

We were in chaos.

The GP kept pushing on.

The paediatrician kept pushing on.

Both were aware of how in decline Eli was.

He was unrecognisable to school. He would not go in.

The early help workers could do nothing with him.

CAMHS did nothing with him.

There was no social worker active.

AND Eli did not get better.

"The World Has Become Very Small"

"You Have To Become Very Small Because The World Is Very Very Big."
—EKW

"Sometimes, I got disappointed with the world and the planets because I didn't have everything I needed. When I was younger.

I think that's why it all broke apart.

You see it was always in me.

I would still be the way I had been acting.

Frustrating.

Sort things put in my mind.

Quite important.

I have a mission.

Versions of people.

Wishes drama magic the gods power to make things happen… Sort everything is out.

Planets that have power.

People keep getting bigger than ever now, more magical than ever. Many different planets of wishes.

Of gods.

Of power.

Of magic.

Many people have different ways… Be ready and prepared the exact way they want.

Do everything you want.

You are there in student ways.

Different planets about you and everything you have.

Not getting it done isn't anything good.

Make it better.

Many different versions of people and what they need on their planets and that is all sorted out we will have anything we need.

Start our new life.

Can't promise how to do it, but I want to do it. No one can stop me.

My music bands understand.

They do the stuff I want to do.

I want to save the ones they couldn't save.

Everyone will have a choice to choose a time to go back to.

Then we can change things now.

If we make a start back then, then we can make it change now.

The professional people didn't understand.

The hospital did a bit.

Andy did, and Ralph did. And ED.

They've got it, and I know you try Mum, but I am annoyed that the CAMHS wrote what they did and the social workers took you to court because that is not what this is about."

—EKW

"I am a person with autism for a reason."

—EKW

The Steam Pot Theory

Early help workers have been called in to provide assistance.

Improve the quality of the family life.
And get Eli back into school.

The idea of early help is to forecast the circumstances and how these could become ameliorated.

Providing help and assistance towards particular groups including the disadvantaged.

This is how it actually went.
It was a torture; it was like watching a car crash in slow motion.

Having to 'get through' these situations with unneeded professionals so that we could get to a better place.

Whilst doors were slamming on us elsewhere, early help workers turned up.
I was assigned a worker.

Without illumination, without knowledge, without a practical history of Eli, she sat in front of me for one and a half hours and read literature about autism.

She asked if Eli had recently been diagnosed.
She told me to remove myself from the situation.

She could not answer, however, when I asked her where I would remove myself.
We have been left to drift on insufferable waters.

What notes have been written have given no justice to the actual real-life scenario. The situation has been downplayed, and the actual suffering has been diminished.

The early help worker assigned to Eli had no idea at all about autism or attention deficit hyperactivity disorder.
I was unsure how she would assist.
But she was someone.
And someone was better than no one.
She handed me leaflets about autism she had pulled from the internet.
She even handed me something I had written myself years ago.

Eli had screamed out that everyone was a fascist and a serial killer, and he was going to rape them.

Having no real understanding of any of these terms.

With this in mind, she handed me rape crisis information.

She told me to put boundaries in place.
She told me that I should send Eli to his room.

Then she met Eli.

He was 5'11"; she was 5'1".
She urgently searched for the exit.
And moved urgently towards the front door.
She spent barely 20 minutes with Eli. A week.

They notice his eyes, the glaze, the anger, the reflection of frustration.
I see them becoming tense and straightening up their backs.

"Are you going to get a hospital for me?" he replies staring through the window ahead.
He does not make eye contact with them.
No, they say; you don't need a hospital.
That's been established, hasn't it?

"So what are you going to do?" I ask.

"We are going to look at strategies to manage Eli," they say.

"Off you go then," I say.

They look down at their phones and notes and pieces of paper they were going to serve me, paper about autism and what it is. How to work with autism.
Lots of words and paper.
And no understanding of autism.
They search for 'strategies' on these pieces of paper.
Look up to the ceiling and on the floor but there is nothing that can help them.
Then they check 'something' on their phones.
They keep looking down at their diagrams with steam pots and lids boiling off.
The answer to everything, for them, lies in these diagrams.
Frantically watching clocks and front doors and a way past Eli.
So they can get out.
They spend most of their time acutely sizing up the room and how to escape if needs must.

They shuffle and look nervous. Then they leave.

They have talked to Eli about steam pots, and lids boiling off.
They give him a colour chart to identify his emotions.
How will this help his emotional decline?

The only way they can perceive this is by calling it anger management.
They talk of boundaries.

But this is more than boundaries, anger and steam pots.
And colour charts.

Eli has fallen apart.
He is no longer the boy we knew.

We are adrift, we need guiding, steering and mooring…and the school and early help workers are adrift with us.
We keep floating aimlessly past each other.

Steam pots and lids boil off, but Eli is in another place, his eyes glazed, his brain tuned into somewhere else.
And they exit hastily. Once more.

They leave, they have now gone.

***

Professionals who anchor hindrance in things at all levels.
Have become so usual, so expected.

"Are they coming for me?"

—EKW

"You see I want people to know me. I want to be famous so that I can get my stuff across. My dreams and the way forward.

I want your parents to come back because I know how much you miss them.

If people can come and see me, then they will listen and then go out and tell everyone else (propagate) and others lots of other people will know what I am on about and try and make it all happen.

I want to get a band and be a part of a band and be famous and go to music college, by the time I am 26 I can get into a music studio and make my album, about nine songs.

Maybe an EP." EKW

Young Carers

My youngest son was only 12 years old when Eli became ill.

He was a registered young carer.
I was now spending all of my time trying to care for Eli.

I could not work.
I could not go shopping.
I could not do anything.

Eli was so badly unwell.

Eli required 24/7 care.
He was not going to school, he was not washing and sometimes not getting out of bed.
And he was insanely violent.

My youngest son observed everything. He was just a child.

He heard me desperately begging, screaming myself into the phone, writing emails of utter despair, for help.
I was running out of people to call.
He was a witness that no one was listening.
No one helped. No one cared.
I could not leave Eli.

My young son took care of all of the household needs, he paid bills, went shopping, bathed his brother, calmed his brother and refused to leave his brother. Even when he came under attack from his brother.

And watched Eli hit me.

My youngest son fed the cats and gave them treatments and vaccines.

There was no social worker to observe this.

Life somehow had to continue at home.

My youngest son's 12th birthday morning was spent chasing after Eli who had bolted from the house.

Police were now accustomed to the calls.
Frustrated there was no other direct assistance.

One officer was filled with sorrow as he looked at the birthday balloons and decorations.
He wished my young son a happy birthday.
Whilst Eli lay crumpled in the corner, rambling incoherently.

My youngest son did the job of the professional. He was Eli's mental health confidante.
He was a psychologist, counsellor, best friend and sympathiser.
He was a brother, advocate and my ally.

He sat amongst the rubble and detriment that Eli had caused, refusing to leave his brother's side.

When Autumn term began, my youngest son was dressed in his uniform ready to begin school at 8:00 am when Eli disappeared into the hills outside our house.
He ran after him, through the wet grass, and mud.
They finally both arrived home again.

My youngest son was just 12.
In a Child in Need meeting, I explained the role of my youngest son.
The 'fixated' learning disability nurse said that my young son was too young to be a carer.

The safeguarding officer from the school assured her that young carers are younger than him.

Much later on, all of the principal services took my youngest son's hard work and efforts, and credited themselves, with his unlimited hard work.

I am on my knees, but I have to hold up Eli and my other children, because no one else will.

We are scared of what has happened so far.

Eli is arrested again because that seems to be the only solution for a 13-year-old boy with autism and ADHD who is mentally unwell.

Myself and my family give unlimited and beyond human capability and care to Eli.

Because no one else will.

But even I am aware that the superhumans have their weaknesses, and at some point, we will break.

No matter how strong a family might be, if no one will hold them up at their most needy, they will crumble.

The learning disability nurse became Eli's object of fixation.

She turned this to her own advantage, and she says she has been working with Eli throughout the entire process.

She wrote in her notes that Eli had some anxiety about the police. She didn't write Eli had been arrested by the police. This changes the whole dynamics.

And she wrote Eli was in control of his behaviours.

She sent some mood diaries to fill in.
I sent them back and said if she wants to know what mood he is in, come to visit him.

***

Small minds only see small things.

"You wouldn't want to know what is happening inside my head."

—EKW

Banging Our Heads Against Those Walls Now

THE 136 SUITE

Being arrested.
Handcuffed. Read his rights. Stuffed into a police van with a cage.
Like a wild, chained animal. Eli was being 'dealt with'.
Locked away.
Thrown into a police cell.
There was no regard for his age, his autism or his learning disability.
He was arrested from places supposed to be keeping him safe.
He spent all night in the cells. Locked in the cells. Denied his freedom.
And the demons chipped away at his brain inside his head.
Antagonising his situation. In custody.
Bewildering the police officers.
Some are only interested in getting him out of the way. None listening to me.
We were all ADHD, remember?

I listened to other people, teachers, professionals and the police; they would never call the police on their children.

Eli was locked in a tiny, empty cell for hours on end.
I was called to say he was not detainable he was fine, and not mentally unwell.

A care package would be provided.

Another care package.

If we look the other way we do not see the problems that are in plain sight.

Eli continued to sink into his mental ocean of darkness and uncertainty, and then hope began to dissipate…

Madness had come to our door some months before.
Insanity had arrived and made a home in our world.

This is Fierce Amongst Chaos and Wisdom

Autism is a lifelong developmental condition, and each person is different, and their autism is unique to them.

It is part of neurodiversity.

It cannot be cured or medicated, and it cannot be grown out.

The condition is vast and unknown and can accompany and be accompanied by other mental health issues.

Eli has ADHD.

Attention Deficit Hyper disorder.

They are both spectrums.

Firstly, we have to understand the spectrum.

What is a spectrum, and why it is used to explain ASD and ADHD?

Bad parenting, trauma within the womb or anything else does not create ASD and ADHD.

We are still learning.

We cannot treat anything without knowing the cause.

The root affliction.

Researching.

We do not know it all.

People with autism do.

People we ADHD do.

It requires patience, empathy, and a great deal of time to be able to provide society with information.

Professionals certainly do not know it all.

There is a volume of truths in greater understanding and compassion and a bigger educational outlook, and then everyone will understand.
Until then the struggle continues.

We do not all have a 'bit of autism' in us.

It is not linear and there is no mild to moderate to severe.
Someone does not have a 'bit of autism' sometimes.
Autism exists, and it is part of the spectrum.

I was thrown off course when I realised how many professionals, including several police officers, knew very little about ASD and ADHD.

This is fierce wisdom amidst chaos and mayhem.

We have to pay attention.
Ego stands in the way of those who do not know, but think they know.

The Painful Continuation

Eli emerged from his bedroom and threw all the rugs from upstairs, downstairs. He began thumping his feet, and tripped me up almost falling down the stairs myself.

"Get me CAMHS!"

He moaned, hanging onto the bottom stair post.

"Get me to the hospital."

He needed both, and he was becoming too violent.

It was too much.

He was thumping and banging, and hitting.

I called the police.

I had no one else to call.

I cried and broke down on the phone.

"Please don't arrest him. He's ill, CAMHS won't help. We were there yesterday… just help, please… please… I don't know what else to do."

The Day Madness Just Became Darker

I have now reached out to every point of call for help.
We have been at this for months.
I'm not sure what else to do.
Where else can I go?

Groups of professionals appear on paperwork, and computer screens, ever-growing and changing, but they are not physically here.

No one comes by, knocks on our door or follows up on phone calls; we are on our own.

Living with the unpredictable.
Doubting our own sanity.

Eli is no longer the boy I know; he has evolved into a sub-species of psychotic mayhem.

Groups of professionals who do nothing cannot be underestimated.
What was actually happening seemed to be irrelevant to the paperwork accruing.

We had entered a long never-ending battle.
I want it to end.

Speak Up

When something needs saying, it is our duty to speak up and when something is wrong or mistaken, we should likewise point it out.

According to the CAMHS learning disability nurse, Eli was in control.

Eli's eyes remained glazed, hair hung in his face, his skin sallowed and became grey, darkening around his eyes.
He spoke unintelligible language. Wrestled with vying demons in his head, his mind.
Monsters that followed him and told him things.
Nothing that made much intelligible sense.

A voice began echoing inside him. A thing.
This became 2. then 3, then multiplied.
They kept replicating.
At a pace, Eli could not understand or keep up with.
His only resource of communication became destruction.
Of anything in his way.
His house, his family, himself, his world.
He tore apart his body with anything that would slice or rip!
He beat himself with anything that would thud.
He ran away from home but the demons chased him. He cried out into the darkness and ran around the house howling.

He threw himself against walls and hurled himself into the garden trees trying to beat and crash the crazy world inside him, out of him.
He yelled and shouted, screamed and sobbed.
He rang the police himself. He called who he thought was the government.

He ran half-crazed and almost naked on the street.

He begged anyone to take him away.

He began to form unlikely scenarios with 'band members'. He wanted a fluffy fur suit to wear. He wanted to get a doctor to take out his mind and replace it. With a fresh new one.
He wanted to go to the hospital because 'band members' were there.

He had conceived a euphoria, and he nurtured this inside his mind.
It lived in his head.
It told him many things.
He needed a concert to sing at so that the audience would hear him and begin propagating his feelings and desires.
He wanted to heal the world because it was hurting. And it throbbed inside Eli.

Everyone took him literally.

He said he was not safe.
At home.

Still, they did nothing. They just wrote he said that.

Still, no one considered the deeper, more unsubstantiated concerns.
Their perceived views of things were so rigid; they could not be altered.

Those I had thought would help, have closed their doors.
I was becoming desperate.

I am swimming in an ocean of far-fetched incredulity.
Unknown territory.
I am so tired.

This is an unchartered journey, I am struggling to see the end in sight, but I had to set my heart on the end goal.
Help.

Hospital, somebody that would take notice.

***

No one is looking for the root cause.
They cannot move forward if they have not addressed the issue before.
Why is Eli like this?

What happened?

No one has investigated. CAMHS have literally done nothing.
There are no social workers.

How can anyone have a correct overview of something when they have not studied the root cause?
Or at least attempted.

Professionals who anchor hindrance in things at all levels have become so usual, so expected.

At the Foot of the Brick Wall

Eli was bruised and bloodied.

ELI was barely a shadow of his former self. His outline of who he had become was rugged and dangerous, terrifying and declining.
His skin was a greyish sallowed rough texture.
His eyes were hollowed, and somewhere within the hollows were his eyes, dim, small, blackening.
His eyes had been taken over by the nightmares inside his brain.
His beard was becoming ragged, and he smelt badly because he did not wash.
He slept in the same clothes.
His state of deterioration was horrifying.
In now rapidly fewer, but calmer moments, I was able to bathe his wounds and tend to them. More often though he would not let me. And would not bathe.
His clothes are unchanged, he said, were reminders. He told me the memories of his pain. He could not let go of them.
Not yet.

Eli unable to make sense of his world or why he was waking up every day, told me that I was just not doing enough to help him.
His tortured mind exhausted him every night.
This pain was his delusion.
This was his daily battle.

Where the monsters arrive surfacing from under the bed, paranoia is the playground for hyper active thoughts.

Madness came into our house when I realised the state of the system meant to be designed to help Eli, was ignoring us.

No one knew us.

They said we saw him as a problem.

But they did not know us.

Eli was so ill.

There were no resources to deal with him.

I have gone up against so many professionals now, and consultants in the community, and am surprised at their arrogance.

They laud their own accomplishments and qualifications.

They are always senior, and managerial, and something with a superior element.

But do nothing to alleviate Eli's agony.

So the nightmare continues.

The New Doctor

There was a new doctor. A locum consultant with CAMHS.
It was mid-February 2018.

This locum psychiatrist consultant admitted there was a big problem.
I saw in her face some grave concern.
I silently determined that she was the one to understand Eli, to know his needs,
to be the one to hospitalise him.
Make him better.

I had begun to crumble away myself, pieces of my own self falling away at the
seams.
I had to hold myself in one piece in front of authorities.
They would simply see this as a weakness.

She wrote some stern letters and demanded he needed hospitalisation.
The locum psychiatrist heard Eli, she listened.
She took calls from Eli every day.
She reviewed his medicine.
By the time the last couple of weeks before the hospital happened, Eli began to
run down to the CAMHS hub, which was just less than a mile away.
Then, a hospital was found.

Rescue

Eli was at the base of the well.
Darkness had now become black.
We could no longer see Eli.
My son was no longer present.

And our home, My house was now a shell.
One stepped over debris to come inside.
My house was hollow, and it echoed.
That was the daily norm.
Social workers could not corroborate.
They were not around.

Generation Hope

It was the weekend of a large national youth Buddhist activity called Generation Hope.

All of my children, friends, partners and other family attended.

It was in Manchester.

All my children except Eli.

He was lying across the floor.

Sometimes motionless.

His head rolled from side to side. His eyes crusted, his hair a crumpled mess of dreadlocks.

CAMHS CRISIS came into our house this weekend.

And they were searching for a tier 4 bed for him.

A place had become available at a local mental health unit in a nearby town.

A ward is reserved for 11 girls and 2 boys.

A CAMHS ward.

Eli packed a bag and stood by the front door.

***

This was the weekend he ran into sub-human temperature half naked holding a knife and the police pursued him.

CAMHS crisis was here.

A bed had been found.

***

On the Tuesday, 20 March 2018, Eli left home.

For hospital.

Apparently for a 24-hour admission.

24 hours!

That afternoon I received a phone call later from the hospital consultant psychiatrist who urgently explained to me what had happened since Eli's arrival. He explained about Eli's behaviour, and how my son had tried to leave the hospital.

He described Eli's all-round appearance.

He had assaulted several members, ripped up books, thrown things around, smashed up shelves and kicked in the doors.

The doctor asked if I could hear the noise in the background.

I could.

A dull heavy thudding.

He explained it was my son.

Kicking the door.

He then explained he had sectioned Eli on a 5(2) under the Mental Health Act.

He told me in his opinion he was extremely unwell and needed further treatment in a more established setting, and they would contain him for now.

But he could not be released back into the community.

That is why he was sectioned under the Mental Health Act.

For the first time fear and worry, pain and heartache, the sleeplessness and overwrought gnawing anxiety that had pulsated through my veins, the whole lot came crashing in on me.

The world around me went foggy, and then swirled, in a few moments.

I could hear the doctor speaking. His voice was penetrating through clouds.

They were listening, and they saw and understood.

The doctor after much conversation then said:

- – Miss Williamson, are you there?
- – Hello.

– Yes, I am here.

– I don't know how you did it.

He described how he and his staff could not believe the state Eli was in.

They were horrified.

That Eli was in the state he was in, and nothing had been done to assist him.

Hospital

A hospital specially designed for autism and mental health needs was offered to take Eli.

I was informed by the local social services to use Eli's disability living allowance to pay for travel to see Eli. They would not pay for travel to see Eli.

No social worker visited the hospital.
Whoever the social worker was had closed Eli's case.
Things have to become so desperate, such a sorrowful state of affairs, things have to get so bad, so disastrous, before any hospitalisation (any care), can be considered.

In the hospital, Eli would begin to receive intricate, profound care, treatment, therapies and remedial approaches that would enable him to recover and begin his life outside the hospital into the community.

The family therapist at the hospital became a professional friend and great counsel to me.
She told me, if you have a child here then you have been through the mill.

The family therapist counselled me, believed in me, understood my 'guilty relief' and added her own terminologies that encouraged me.
I could let down my guard, it was with her I could cry, sob and release my hurt and pain.
And everything that was geared toward what lay ahead.
She prepared me for what could happen afterwards.

The mental health hospital gave credence to Eli's state of mind, his lack of ability to make sense of the real world, his delusional aggressive mind and behaviours that stemmed from this, and that he might refuse treatment.

It appeared from the shrouds of suffering that we had become so accustomed to, and it reigned during Eli's life for the next 18 months. A lodge was available on hospital grounds for families and carers to stay in whilst visiting our children. It was free.

A hospital is an artificial setting. It cannot last forever.
And hospitals like these are forever under scrutiny.
More often than not, they close.

It was a remedial centre and hub of nurturing activity around Eli.
If we do not value the child, how can we move forward?
If we cannot offer help, assistance, hope and belief, we are not valuing the child.

In retrospect now, I do not think anyone can prepare a parent for what will happen after the hospital.

Mental Health Section

It is a momentous time when the Mental Health Act is introduced into a person's life.

In our case, it was welcomed.

When a person is detained, also known as sectioned under the Mental Health Act, it means they can be hospitalised and treated against their wishes.

Without their agreement.

Usually, this is because they are in urgent need of treatment for a mental health disorder, and could pose a risk to themselves and others.

Therefore, they require removal from society.

They can stay in the hospital until the consultants or a mental health tribunal decide otherwise. Families can visit, and generally, this is nothing dissimilar to any other type of hospital visit.

Treatment plans, concerns and worries for all kinds of things are discussed in the hospital with staff.

Mental health staff in the hospital vary and are normally extremely different from workers in the community.

Their role is to assist extremely mentally unwell people and take care of their needs, in this critical situation.

Eli was originally on Section 5(2) which gave doctors the ability to detain him in hospital for up to 72 hours.

During this time, he received an assessment that decided what should happen next.

And it was decided further detention under the Mental Health Act was necessary.

Eli received a Section 2 which evolved into Section 3.

Section 3 was renewed every six months until Eli left the hospital.

Police, mental health advisors, social workers, the GP and many other professionals can voice their concerns about the patient prior to hospitalisation.

In Eli's case, this did not happen.

Because he was still in the community.

Courts and police can section immediately if that person appears to be at risk to themselves or anyone else in the community.

I am still baffled about this part.

Eli had been at substantial risk in the community.

But this had been ignored.

The Mental Health Act is structured into many sections, hence why the word, section is used, and it is a detention under the Mental Health Act.

It is not prison and the patients are not criminals.

Things had become so bad this is what happened to Eli.

This area of his life is often downplayed. By professional services around him in the community.

However, services around Eli had done nothing to prevent hospitalisation, and neither had they offered any assistance, to secure his safety or his mental health well-being. No matter what they tried to say later on.

It was in the hospital he received the care he desperately needed.

It took 21 months.

And a lifetime beforehand, it seemed to get him there.

And Eli's mental health detention actually kept him very safe, as the following chapters will demonstrate.

"When I heard that when I was 18, I could do what I wanted. Apart from bad stuff, I really loved adults."

—EKW

Part Two
Mental Health Hospital

It was painful to watch Eli in the hospital.

He was one of my children.

No parent wants to watch their child suffer, be humiliated, fall apart, be arrested or be ignored.

Be hospitalised.

I juggled home life and visiting Eli.

Sometimes, I brought the family to see Eli.

Sometimes, it was just me.

There was a special lodge, free to families who were visiting. We could stay there.

Eli broke down and was built up.

He broke down some more and was built up even more.

He said intolerable things, screamed and shouted and was supervised by two people all of the time in the beginning.

He sometimes went into seclusion.

His monitoring went down to one person.

This meant he was watched all of the time.

Eventually, he did not need monitoring, but this was a process of months.

The care plan around Eli, like all patients was tailor-made to his requirements.

Which differed greatly for each patient.

The hospital stood in spacious luscious green grounds.

Each room for the patients had their own bathroom, and they were encouraged to do laundry.

There was a special kitchen area where the patients could order whatever they wanted and make meals, treats and anything they wanted.
This happened with supervision.

Community leave was granted to see how Eli would behave, and in the first instances, it was very touch and go.
Sometimes with staff and sometimes inviting me too.
He would struggle with boundaries and off-limits behaviour.
He was still ill, but he was being medicated and monitored.
There were occasions we all had to abort the mission.
Other times, he would take his shoes off, and I would carry them as he walked barefoot through the towns.

We persevered.

There were CETR and other independent reviews and a mental health tribunal because he was on section.

There were Continuous meetings, CPAs (Care Programme Approaches) and these involved all of the care Eli was receiving.

Local CAMHS were invited plus myself, Eli and many other hospital professionals, OT, psychologists, SALT, etc.
Advisors, registrars.
Eli received intricate care.

My son was in capable hands, and at last, he was recognised for having broken down in the first instance.

It was interesting to see CAMHS from community in the hospital, looking a little washed out and sheepish.

Firstly, he received a diagnosis of psychotic disorder.
Later this evolved into schizoaffective disorder.

There were CETR and other independent reviews and a mental health tribunal because he was on section.
A social worker did become involved, but this was a reticent, slow indifferent worker who kept talking about being a returning social worker.

I did not leave my son's side and often arrived with the rest of our family.
Every 4-5 days I visited him, and called him three times a day, or he called me.

I juggled caring for my other children and getting on with my other duties in life.

Trains were sometimes not regular, and there could be long waiting on station platforms through all weathers.

I was not reimbursed by the local authority.

I had for some reason believed the social services put children first.
I had believed this meant, valuing the child.

I brought Eli all of his necessary things. Whilst in hospital I was still to provide his clothes, toiletries, snacks and drinks, books, DVDs, gadgets and anything else he might need.
And use his money to travel and visit him.

It was expensive.
Especially looking after a family at home and not always being at home when they finished school and college.

***

A part of Eli's journey back to recovery were home leaves, which eventually turned into overnight leaves.

These became Eli's 'happy ever after'.
He made it.
Trial and error.

But he got there.
At home, he behaved impeccably.
And he was getting better.
A better version of himself.
Better than he ever was.

***

The cruel reality of things is that it must all get so bad, so outstandingly awful and horrible before the circumstances around the young person can change.

When the world has already made up their minds about someone like Eli, the route forward is a blizzard of agony and confusion.

"To be like me, you have to get very small because it's all so very big."

—EKW

When darkness had descended over Eli; his lighter self was fading fast.

Inside Eli, there had raged a monster.
A monster Eli could not fight; he could not retaliate.
A monster that grew and became angrier, hungrier and vengeful.
The monster exploited the vulnerability of my son, so young, with all of his outstanding special needs.

Aggression took hold and violence entered Eli.
This was the only language left that Eli could use.
And it hurt.

But one day in hospital someone lit the light and held it up, and he began to stand up and feel his way forward.

Off Limits Without Boundaries

Mental health is like society.
It is fragile and needs nurturing.

We cannot just assume because we live in a democracy that everything will be diplomatic.
We are looking to these very bodies of community, the social and societal precepts that hold up our structures and take care of us.
Those that pertain to anything concerned with social conditions.
Community, social living, ethics.
Equality, happiness, communal living. Human rights.
Everyone becomes affected.
Mental health is fragile.

If it is not looked after, taken care of and tended to, it will break.
Darkness can descend from all areas.
It can cloud over and cover like black shrouds in almost every area of life.

The mind alters, nothing makes sense, and those around you have no meaning.
Psychosis is off limits without boundaries and stands alone in its unique, powerful and still very misunderstood spectrum.
Where no one and nothing can alleviate anything, the professional seniors in mind medicine are required.

Because ignoring it will not make it go away.

"The violence…it was always there; it just came out now."

—EKW

The Truth

A truth half undone is a half-undone truth.
It serves no purpose, and it isn't the truth.

If it doesn't begin with the truth, it cannot begin anywhere, at all.

One cannot invent the truth; it has to be recalled.

It is interesting to learn things about yourself and your family from professionals who never worked with us, said by people who never knew us and/or do not know us.
I have found it to be quite revealing about the professionals concerned.

I am still astonished at the lengths a professional will go to, to try and elaborate something they never gave us in the first place.

Lies beget lies, and eventually, the liar is found out tripping over their own follies.
Using a series of untruths to get out of difficult situations.
Situations they themselves got us all into; situations they lied about in the first place.

We cannot talk about things in detail we have never experienced.

"When are you getting me out of here, Mum?"

—EKW

Discharge and Service Speculation

Service specifications were released by Eli's hospital.

The purpose was to suggest a way to bring Eli back into community life and back home forever.

So the suggestion was that a nearby placement that could cater to Eli's needs would be the way forward.

The concern from the hospital was that our country did not have the best most current record for care services, and therefore I might not be able to care for Eli on my own, without resources.

This was guidance in place.

The worry was that if Eli became unwell again, he could return to the pre-hospital situation, without positive resources or services that would provide for him, and given his history, support him.

The social services were now required, and social services workers were sent in.

Their principal aim was supposed to be to make sure a placement was found, as stipulated in the specifications by the hospital.

However, this is not quite how it went.

A social worker was assigned to the task of social working Eli and searching for a placement.

She never turned up to meetings.

She made excuses for her shoddy; poorly composed reports.

She said a majority of her written-up work was done late at night.

And her 'mistakes' were typos.

Dates and events were assorted and mixed up, and none of it made any sense, and the way it was written was a literary disaster.

There had been a genogram (sent out to me by an early help worker) that revealed a completely different family.
Supposedly the support family network.

The mental health tribunal was postponed in late 2018 because the social worker just did not turn up.
It had to be re-arranged.
She appeared disinterested.
The tribunal judge took her to task.

The LA seemed incapable of finding a placement.
It had now been months.

Eli was continuing to improve steadily and was coming on frequent home leaves, and overnight leaves.
This meant whilst on Section (MHA), he was able to be at home and in the community and do whatever we wanted to do together as a family without hospital support.

One day a placement was found.
Located miles away from our home. They were that far away; they took a plane to visit the hospital.
When Eli was not there, he was at home on an overnight home leave.

However, they said they could meet his needs, according to paperwork.

No one knows why they took a plane.
Perhaps it indicated how far away they were.

Further research demonstrated it would take at least three trains and several taxis to arrive at this placement.

Trains can mean delays, leaves on the track, cancellations, and if we are reliant on a relay of trains to get us to a destination, one delay can set everything off course.

It would take all day to get to this placement hundreds of miles away, by train. And it would be expensive.

So I said no, Eli said no, all-round staff thought it was a bit far away.
The social worker left.

The Objection

This placement was not close or in alliance with the service specifications.
However, this did not matter to the social services.

I objected because of the distance and gave multiple reasons why.
This also did not matter to the social services.

It had become all about Eli going into this placement.
Come what may.

It was not about what was best for him, or what Eli wanted, and he had been clear about what he wanted.
It was not about his mental health situation or the egregious background before the hospital.
In fact, this was nothing to do with Eli.

Any objections were conveniently unheard by the social services.

They were adamant Eli was going to the placement.

I had said Eli could come home.
However, led only by paperwork, the social services local authorities were insistent and unyielding.

Another social worker arrived.
She parroted the insistence of the local authority, and herself was obdurate.

She insisted that Eli's younger brother could be potentially at risk if Eli returned to the family home.

She did not know us.
She did not know Eli's youngest brother.
At risk from who, we were unsure.

This was the same young brother who counselled Eli through his darkest hours.

Eli's Patient advocate explained and advocated Eli's rights.

The hospital social worker quoted a few human rights too.

Eli was and is protected by various different sections of legislation.
And general human rights.
These highlight the importance of his voice being heard in any decision about his future and care.
Eli had stated clearly and continuously to me, his patient advocate, his solicitor, his nurses, the RC, and many other professionals that he did not wish to go to a placement far away from his home.
He explained that he wanted and needed to be close to his family for him and us to have maximum contact and where he can continue to benefit from the close supportive relationships that he enjoys with all of us.
This is crucial to his well-being.
Eli does not thrive away from home, far away.

And Eli requires long, intricate transition periods.
Transition is personal and unique to the individual.

We, his family require detailed information about how things will work out.
Family contact, home visits, and a date to return home for good.

The social services were not listening and had no desire to listen.
Whatever I was trying to desperately say, was now inconsequential to them.
Where they had been nonchalant, uninterested and perfunctory before Eli's time in the hospital, they were now leading the way.
And not just that, they were bulldozing their way through.
And it was their way.

No crossroads, no junctions, no stopping, no thinking. Whatever I was trying to desperately say, was now inconsequential to them.

This epoch would prove to be perhaps the most contentious moment of Eli's life to date. And a vivid picture of what the local authority will do to achieve their goals.

Part Three
Hemlock and Disaster

When does protocol become more important than the actual needs and happiness of the young person?

The social worker did not answer, respond, communicate, or explain thoroughly anything.
She was on leave, in a meeting, not at her desk, on sick leave.
She was always somewhere else, but not in the place we needed her to be.

Her role seemed to be to coerce me into accepting the one and only placement they had found, for Eli.

I objected to the placement because it was too far away.

She continued to repeat that a placement had now been found and that was that.

***

I was offered no other alternative placements to view.
I strongly objected.

The distance was irrelevant to the local authority.

***

The LA have now informed me they are really worried about Eli.

"...for goodness sake, let me make my machine, get it shipped across over here, and it will change everything. I'm the chosen person, next. They have to listen; they are going to have to..."

—EKW

The Practice Supervisor

I was summoned into the social services offices during the summer of 2019.

My fractious relationship began with the practice supervisor.

He referred to my objections about the placement as reaching a Stalemate.
He referred to me as, 'The Impasse'.
He threatened me that I would be taken to court if I did not go and see the placement, and if I did not accept it, they would take further action to get Eli placed there. A care order.

I had been looking, with other professionals, for other closer placements.

The practice supervisor refused to confer with me, he was inflexible and stubborn. He was determined to see things through, in his way.

He had enough conviction that he would succeed in his goal and that nothing was going to stop him.

I learned later he had been working behind my back, liaising with the 'far away' placement to get Eli placed by the end of September or early October 2019.

The matter of Eli's mental health or even his MH section, seemed to be of little concern.

It was no longer relevant that the social services had done nothing to accommodate my son or my family when we had gone through such turbulence previously.

For some reason, the tunnel vision, all but blinded by their own vision, was about putting Eli in the ONLY placement that had been found.

That was it.

It was a macabre and dark time.
Things were moving along at the practice supervisor's directive.

There was no social worker.
There was never a social worker.

He was a stiff-necked, unkind man, and he commandeered the ship now.
He had never met Eli.
He told me he probably never would.
He had taken over and told me that if a care order was sought, then my children at home would be investigated.

As things were, and with my objection to the placement, and the supervisor refusing to acknowledge that this could cause great unease and mental health concerns for my son.
This now meant that my family were at risk.

I was his obstacle, his impasse.

And he became my oppressor.
I was the perpetrator, and he was my aggressor.
This had become solely about putting Eli into a residential placement.

It was further than parenting, or Eli's best interests, it was bureaucracy.
Paperwork and politics.
Protocol.
That took over.

More than that…

It was war.

"First you bring the autism; then you use the autism."

—EKW

Oppression forces people down.
Because we are different.
And because of who we are, and what we represent.
Our way of life is perhaps outcast or outside the usual conventions, so it becomes
a threat to others.
We cannot be controlled you see.

We have become a menace.

If those supposed to be responsible for society, and taking care of the vulnerable,
told the truth, this would open up an unmistakable possibility to the rest of us.

If they give rise to us to make choices, that will not serve their interests.
So they keep us 'down', oppressed and make us angry.
But heed caution:
When we become angry, we can be controlled.
Do not get angry.1
Breathe deeply, listen, let their words fall softly to the ground.
Use humour and conversation. Smile. Hear them. Do not argue.

The Social Worker

The social worker found her way back to her desk.
She delivered by hand to me, an Intent of Court Proceedings on 9 September 2019 to my front door.

I was at home talking to Eli on the phone.

By this time, I had legal counsel. They were trying to talk with the local authority.

The social worker diluted any attempt by me to make conversation between her and me.

She disregarded anything that went before, she had no time or interest in Eli's history and used obsolete, patronising terminology about Eli.
She frequently wrote things out of context.
She disrupted my now-settled family and concentrated only on getting Eli into the far-away placement.

This became the entire and sole focus of her services.

Her needle was caught in the groove.
She was a broken record.
She kept saying the only placement was the one hundreds of miles away.

Her words were well rehearsed.
She attacked my questions, spoke over me, inhibited me, and then turned things around for me.

She stated I could not care for Eli, and this tore apart my credibility.

***

When parents are unheard, we are tarred, with the same brush.

We all exist together in the same crowd, under a thick, dark sky.

It is simply bureaucracy, ticking boxes and an inability for the local authority social services to see ahead.
Paperwork blocks the way.

The social worker seized the opportunity to cause ill feelings when rumours of the hospital closure circulated.
There was no fixed date.

We, the families were all informed.

The social worker could not control the date of closure.
There was No Fixed Date.

NO FIXED DATE.

***

The court proceedings paperwork talked about the LA being 'worried' about my son.

They wanted Eli in the proposed placement. The only placement.

Or to find him a placement, and if unsuccessful, was there anyone else that could look after my son?
They were talking about safeguarding my son…from me.

***

The situation at this stage had become ludicrous. They wanted to go halves on Parental responsibility.

This was purposefully orchestrated to take Eli out of my parental care.

With an interim care order.

It made absolutely no sense at all.

And was far removed from the circumstances of 2017.

I could not recall the social services being 'worried' about Eli in 2017.

Yet here we were on the verge of court proceedings.

***

It had become so convoluted and mixed up that I think the local authorities lost themselves.

***

I had to continue visiting Eli, pretend everything was OK, allay the worries of my family, and try and overthrow the mainstream paradigm of bureaucracy.

I was bewildered about the concerns of special needs and vulnerable people, those with disabilities and learning difficulties.

But as with all things I had to find the right time, no one listening.

This was not the right time.

The social services had become hostile and tried to overturn me at every stop.

They attacked from all sides.

However, I knew not to feed their intentions, instead to move around them, and smile.

Using my words carefully and with thought.

To act in a way, they did not expect of me.

To challenge them, intelligently.

With compassion and humour.

Above all else tell the truth.

Someone had to tell the truth.

A Great Leader

A great leader is one who is unable to be identified.

They go on ahead and assess the new territory, when they are satisfied, they beckon the rest of the pack.

They lead others to victory. They put themselves last.

Their concern and achievement are with those dependent upon them. They serve the people.

Those are the attributes of a great leader.

I was not dealing with great leaders.

They Had Me over a Barrel,
One Arm Behind My Back

A legal situation was now brewing.
Interim care order sought.
The local authority cauldron was bubbling heartily.

Things escalated, very quickly, and we were going to court.

On 13 September 2019, I had just come back from an overnight visit with Eli, when I was immediately summoned to my solicitor's office.

I turned around and found myself staring down the barrel of an interim care order.
The social services/local authority had declared war on me.
They were taking me to court on the following Monday morning.
16 September 2019.
It was urgent.

My solicitor wanted my instruction and informed me that the LA had told her that Eli's hospital was closing next week on September 18.
It was now September 13 and about two hours before office closing time. Friday afternoon.

They wanted an interim care order to place Eli in the Residential Placement.
They wanted to achieve this in two days.

Their plan was to receive a care order from the County Court on Monday the 16 September 2019 and have Eli transported from the hospital to the placement by the 18 September 2019.

Two days.

Without preparation, without transition.
They were planning in two days to transport my vulnerable son, Eli, from one part of the UK to another.
They wanted to remove him from the hospital and place him elsewhere.

This would mean my son, Eli, would be placed in unfamiliar surroundings.
For anyone, this can be unsettling.

For someone with special needs, and several learning disabilities, for Eli, it would become a living hell.

It would be the undoing of all the remedial work accomplished by those dedicated members of staff at the hospital over the past 18 months.
And by us, his family.

Eli could be at further risk of being arrested, in the hands of staff who did not understand him or his circumstances.

My family had not left Eli's side.

The possible violent repercussions and aftermath of this had become overwhelmingly unbelievable.

I had been thrown against a brick wall.

The local authority formally had remained benighted and unpolished and uninterested.
Were now in ambush.
I was being taken to court.
I had been pulled over a barrel.
It was legal, no getting out of it.
The supervisor had kept his side of things.
And all of this mayhem was in place because of him.

I was now part of a train wreck in slow motion.
Unable to control it.

Eli was unaware, and I had no idea how to tell him.
Or if he would ever trust me again.

Working the Extra Mile

In the two hours left to me on that working day, 13 September 2019, I had to work fast.

On a Friday afternoon, I had to run.

I cannot remember my instructions to my lawyer.

I babbled something to her and dragged across town the enormous folder she handed me 'about Eli'.

She told me I must turn up, at 9:00 am at court Monday morning and the local authority would pay for public transport.

There was no public transport before 9:00 am, so I had to take a taxi.

This cost £40.

In 2019.

So I paid out of my carer's allowance.

This was £67 a week at the time.

***

First of all, I called the hospital and told them everything.

They were bemused because I had just left them that morning.

And they were further amused to hear that their hospital was closing.

Because it wasn't.

I managed to speak with the RC consultant and the hospital manager.

They gave me this same information and provided it in writing too.

By this time my solicitor had gone home.

So, I sent it on to her secretary.

On Friday evening, I spoke with the placement principal.

She informed me she had been liaising with the practice supervisor and sent me her emails.

From this I deduced the practice supervisor had been working behind my back to get Eli into this placement anyway. He had envisaged Eli at the placement in early October 2019.

The placement principal informed me that her placement could not take Eli as an emergency.

So they would not be able to take him straight away.

This meant if the care order was provided, the local authority would effectively have no placement in which to place Eli.

And this was the entire point of the interim care order.

And this fiasco of an Urgent Court Hearing.

***

Next, I demanded the practice supervisor organise transport to take me to the placement over the weekend.

He tried to dissuade me from going.

He said none of the mental health staff and teachers would be there over the weekend.

I was adamant and told him to get transport.

I told him he was on loudspeaker and the rest of my family were listening to our conversation.

He reluctantly arranged everything for me.

Off we went the next day.
A very long journey, five hours in the taxi one way.
I accepted the placement.
And I told the placement why.
That was that part done.

***

The local authority had no jurisdiction to take Eli from the mental health hospital whilst he was in the mental health section.

If the RC refused to rescind the mental health section, which she probably would, the local authority would then have to seek out a mental health tribunal judge.

Another hearing.
This would take time.

More than two days.
The practice supervisor had not thought things through.
The hospital was not closing on the date he had provided.

So we had Eli's mental health section preventing him from being removed from the hospital by the local authority.

The placement themselves were unable to take him immediately.

The hospital was in fact not closing on the date the LA had issued on the urgent court hearing.

I noticed also that the local authority had also used my social media name, which I never used legally.
One wonders why they did that.

Transition with someone as complex as Eli has to be choreographed.
Careful, unique and tailor-made, it is essential to get it just right.

I knew the local authority social services could be difficult, and bull-headed, but this took things onto a strange, and frightening new level.

There appeared to be little consolation from the local authority about the effect this was having on the rest of my family.

The Urgent Court Hearing

As I sat in court on Monday, 16 September, having let go of over £40 one way on a taxi, composed as I might have appeared, I was in utter turmoil inside.
But I could not let down my guard, or let my vulnerability show to the local authority.
Or the court.
Or the judge.

***

We are in very dark, cold places, when there is no one left to turn to.
When those in power are meant to be helping, those canons of society meant to be in place for the vulnerable and those in need have now taken over.

When the bullies are let loose and allowed to be so habitually cruel, where can we go?

Who will listen?
Who will help us?

Where is the justice?

How does this put children first?

County Court
16 September 2019, 9:00 am

The social worker was apparently unaware of any of the ensuing debacle.
And here she was, with her supervisor having to stand face to face with me in the courtroom.

In court, there was a lot of waiting around and a great deal of talking.
Lawyers talking, reading, debating, coming back, explaining things to their clients, going off for more meetings and discussing things more.

My daughter recalls later I was shaking.
I was apparently literally trembling.

There was a lot of talking, a lot of coming and going by lawyers and barristers.

Things were a mess now, but any other alterations at this stage would certainly get the fireworks ignited way too early and most likely in the wrong direction.

The solicitor for Eli was someone I had never met before.

Eli had no idea he was being represented by this unknown commodity.

The court is just strange.
I will never understand how it works to represent someone who has never been met.

***

What transpired is that the judge was less than impressed.

Once in the courtroom, I had to listen to the local authority lawyer pronounce things wrongly and get the name of the placement wrong.
There was to and fro about dates and times.

The judge stated he had already had an almost identical situation with the local authority and another family, again with wrong and erroneous information on hand.

He was unhappy about the urgent hearing no longer being urgent.

And the information was intermittent, out of date and mostly now irrelevant.
But with all the obstacles in front of the local authority, and them having no clear evidence about how things would pan out, no placement to effectively put Eli, it was less than satisfactory.

He wanted to see what progress had been made in the meantime in terms of placements and so on.

A great deal of the commentary during court became an incoherent garrulous noise.
I had been so nervous and traumatised and was now exhausted, and these were words beyond Eli and his world, and what was required, were just sounds.
We were in a different paradigm.

The judge commended me for my efforts over what must have been a very long and tiring weekend.

He was not happy with the local authority and reprimanded them.

I have never seen so many people exit a courtroom so quickly, and the local authority did exactly this.

I took my time.

Liaised with my solicitor, everything was fine; there was no care order; I remained fully responsible for Eli.

There was no need to panic.

I even made eye contact with the practice supervisor.
His facial expressions changed several times staring back at me, in a few seconds.
I just kept staring at him.
He knew what my eyes were telling him.
He knew what I was saying.

My face said everything he needed to know.

He moved off and out of sight quickly, never to be seen again.

Carers

We are the carers, and our beds rest in muddy waters.
The senseless and the bizarre are not strangers to the life of a carer.
Putting up with professionals is an unfortunate norm.
The unpredictable is the norm.
The unreasonable is the norm.

Outside the boundaries is the norm.
Far from the suburbs of mainstream is the norm.
Reading things that have not happened is the norm.

Discovering something in a report about our dependent that happened once, for half an hour in an entire year of 365 days, is the norm.

The rest of the year being dismissed or whispered about is the norm.

Reading spurious, sparse reports and assessments, and copies of essays about how things have moved along with Eli that have no rudimentary essence to the reality of things, is the norm.
And watching them get passed along to other professionals, senior officials, and so forth, is the norm.

We are more than our role; we become everything that is not provided by those supposed to provide.
We do not sleep, and we always provide.
We are not paid.
We do everyone else's job.

We are the centrepiece and the linchpin.

The Truthteller, the record keeper and the entire set of notes.

We know it has to begin with the truth.

We hope one day it will.

But, for now, there is no truth.

Half-baked truth, half undone truth.

But that is not true.

Those of us who are presumed to not be conforming to the mainstream expectations or are not quite by the book, are ousted.

Rejected. Unheard.

We live differently.

We are different.

We are no less, and no more.

We are simply not mainstream; we do no wrong and cause no harm.

We accept the poor treatment because this is what we have come to know.

What is expected of us keeps changing, there are no provisions and no documentations.

We just get on with things.

We care.

There is no guidebook.

Rules are set by those who have no idea either.

Whatever we were meant to be, is so much more than the vocabulary they will ever be able to find.

Carers are in everything, and we will be in everything, we are always there and defend until achievement.

And we will keep chipping away at the system, until the system, changes.

We are not outlaws.

We are different.

We do not stop.

We are exhausted.

We dive in after other families in the same predicament and try to help sort things out.

We share.

Offer shelter.

Shake off rebuke.

We are simply outside the norm.

We are the carers.

Part Four
Third Hospital and the Residential School
Court of Protection

Court of Protection: is a protective area that supports the rights of the vulnerable.
They direct the local authority.
The placement, the family.
The reports rendered should explain who Eli is.
The history gives some idea of who he is and what he has been through.

The Court of Protection is a superior court of record.
Its function is to have jurisdiction over the overall welfare of people who lack mental capacity.
And have difficulty making decisions for themselves.

It was created under the Mental Capacity Act 2005.

DOLS
Deprivation of Liberty

The DOLS order details everything necessary and the judge gives directions on how to execute these actions.

That is what is meant to happen.

Both the DOLs and the COP are there to protect people who do not have the capacity and have possibly spent time under the Mental Health Act on Section.

***

"Stop restarting the pain."

—EKW

After the fiasco of the urgent court proceedings, things did not get better.

Eli remained in the hospital that did not close on the date the local authority had provided.
Although it would be closing.

A place had to be found for Eli meantime.

However, the local authority had not been able to find any other placement apart from the far away one.
They held meetings without me and kept talking about finding Eli a temporary placement.

The social worker still maintained I could not care for Eli.

The practice supervisor had been replaced, I do not know what happened to him, however, thankfully ousted from his position, she had a new arrival.

And there would be another after that.

We all wondered where the temporary placement would come from.

It appeared that my son, Eli, was represented predominantly by the local authority.

They conveniently left out most of relevant details about Eli's past.

And most of the relevant details about Eli's past.

The local authority continued to use their rhetorical vocabulary, and their notes had huge gaping holes in them.

They seemed to have some intimidating power.

And this, for now, would unfortunately lead the way.

***

The abrupt and fierce arrival of the social services took us on a route which veered way off from the direction of mental health and instead it became about learning disabilities.

Which they kept saying was diagnosed.

Notes are now provided by the local authority social services about Eli, ourselves…his family, and his background.

It is a dismal time in anyone's life to discover we are being spoken for by a body of people who could not be bothered with us in the first place.

Don't give them your information they will only make it their own.

The Third Hospital

Another mental health hospital was suggested and procured for Eli.
Until the placement became available.

At least there was no more talk of temporary placements.

This particular hospital could not cope with Eli's autism, nor his ADHD, and asked me to debrief them and help re-educate them in how best to approach things.

Staff had become worried Eli was not eating.
This was because of the new surroundings.
Transition.
And because of the quality of their food.
Hospital food.

He was used to his own kitchen to make and cook things.
It was different here.
The whole hospital was different.
It was vast.
Many floors and the only way to arrive at the ward was by a large, windowless lift, which rocked and racketed.
I do not like lifts, and this challenged me for the three months Eli was there.

The social worker had been approached about how Eli had provided his food before.
Social workers are always approached long before the parents are.
Because it is believed by all that the social worker has been known to the subject/service user/patient for a good deal of time.

The hospital was unaware of the musical chairs situation with social workers.

They are relied upon to give up-to-date, important information.
Because they are the ones who apparently, know.

Who promote the well-being of the young person.

She did not know Eli and appeared much more concerned with her time in office.

She continued to argue with me and spoke over me.
And conveniently hung up on me because there were problems on the line.

When I disputed things written about me in the social services report she told me it was a hospital report.

She used flamboyant, flowery writing, and used too many words to describe a situation, she had not been a part of.

Instead of writing, Eli had planned and prepared most of his meals in the other hospital, in the specially adapted kitchen for patients, for his oncoming week.
She wrote that short term meal plans were in place for forth coming days.
What is a forthcoming day?

Eli told her he wanted a fur suit.
She misheard and wrote in her reports. Aversu."
I was intrigued to discover that when asked, she provided me a description of what she believed it to be.

She had told me that she had a really good relationship with Eli.
She enjoyed some of the same music as him.
I repeated this to Eli, who replied that he had no idea who she was.

When he did realise who she was his dislike of her intensified.
He held her responsible for putting him into the residential placement and moving him out of the other hospital.
Further away from home.

To know autism, ADHD and the accompanying mental health conditions is to live it, day in and day out.

To know all of this is much more than textbooks.

To know mental health in young people and ASD and ADHD and other neurodiverse conditions is to lose your own ego, and apply that concentration on the person, not yourself.

To be a social worker is much more than rhetoric and paperwork.

But that is what we had, and we had to get used to it.

She frequently turned up at the hospital without warning.

She never announced her arrival, and everything had to stop.

Eli had to hang up his phone calls with me, and cease whatever he was doing because her presence was in the building.

It suited the hospital for Eli to come home on home leaves.

It was easier for them.

The social worker did not visit him on his home leaves.

To be honest I am not sure she even knew most of the time he was coming on home leaves.

It is not my job to inform her. It is her job as a concerned employee to serve Eli's best interests.

I was allowed to take Eli out of the hospital grounds, on my own.

This is whilst he remained in MH section.

We often went to the huge supermarket opposite.

There was a large, famous departmental store nearby too. It was nearing Halloween, Christmas and our birthdays. Many celebrations.

Eli loved this time of year.

We walked about in the community.

Through the streets on our own, together.

He was happy, and we purchased whatever he wanted.

Eli very much looked forward to going out, so he could eat a proper lunch.

And he ate his fill.

We tried perfumes and creams and became models for expos; looked at expensive sitting rooms and the garden section.

Back in the hospital grounds which were extensive, we sat in the old bowling green, in the hut, and I let him listen to music on YouTube.

Wildlife was abundant, and sometimes, we would see foxes that trotted quite close by to us.

Most of the grounds were beautiful, with luscious greenery and some unkempt gardens that reminded me of classical novels, and secret gardens, some of the grounds were submerged under water because of torrential rainfall.

Eli's many overnight leaves were hugely successful.

There were plenty of different activities to do. Swimming, the cinema, sometimes just being at home in familiar, loving surroundings, and Eli ate what he liked. He was better; he was well; he was an improved incredible version of himself.

In hospital I provided what snacks I could, but it was often just crisps and biscuits, pain au chocolat, and squash.

He no longer had the possibility of cooking his own food. So this had to make do.

According to the social worker, he was eating well.

I am unsure if she would be happy if her children were only eating snacks all day.

These were unusually good times: the journey to the third mental health hospital was nightmarish though and there were frequent train delays, it was cold often very damp, and dark, and it took all day, a long tiring day to get to Eli and back home again.

Many cancellations, and long, cold waiting on platforms filled with commuters, and tired travellers.

But it was worth it, to get to Eli.

The original commotion made by the local authority social services, about interim care orders, me not caring for Eli, him being at risk or whatever it was they were spinning, made little sense now.

Eli was walking around with just me in plain open public.

And he was coming home, overnight on leaves.

Multiple evenings.

No one seemed alarmed.

Failure is clear to see.

There is a divide between ignorance and stupidity.

Yet this intensified as the rest of our journey ahead through the system continued.

And the system became divided amongst many more professionals.

At this stage, it was still really to our advantage to just go along with things. That is how ridiculous things were.

***

The only ones who are oblivious to any failings are those who have set things in motion from disorder.

***

It is beyond human possibility to keep our heads above water and maintain decorum, keeping things as they are supposed to be, amidst utter disorder.

And the services provide disorder.

They work from chaotic scripts. They have written these.

In time they will not be able to make sense of their own work, because of disordered, disarray.

Things have been allowed to get out of control because there were no clear logistics in the first place.

And it is becoming clearer to me now, that professionals and members of staff, everywhere, are receiving their information and advice about Eli from others who know almost nothing about Eli and his circumstances.

The non-informed, leading the non-informed.

The Maximum Family Contact Clause

I had been promised maximum family contact.

There was no clear description of what this would entail.

I was simply informed we would have maximum family contact when Eli went into residential placement.

This was vague and changeable.

Social services were unaware and uninterested in the impact all of this was having on the rest of my family.

There was no clarity on how we would travel to Eli, how many people in the family could go and where we would stay.

Only we could see him every other week at the placement and transport and lodging would be provided.

This now had to be achieved by the services, and it was going to be expensive.

I told them so.

How arduous the journey would be.

Saying public transport is one thing; taking it is quite another ordeal.

Our lodgings were in fact one room at the edge of a motorway, in a motel lodge for motorists.

The one room that was provided, was considered satisfactory in the local authority opinion for two female adults and a teenage boy.

They also informed me if I wanted more rooms or more people, I could always pay for the more.

I had not been informed originally by the social services of this.

We were transported by taxi.

***

It is just the pin that keeps the grenade intact.

The Placement

The placement did not know most of Eli's intricate background.
The social services had not provided all the necessary information.
They had not been informed about his original breakdown, the intense police activity, the police arrests, Eli's hospital home leaves, and overnight home leaves.
They seemed to be under the impression I had very young children.
The social services had been clear, I could not look after Eli.

I was fully responsible for Eli and there was no joint parental responsibility with the local authority.
I was nevertheless treated as through there was a care order in place.

The information the placement had was that the last hospital in Manchester was the only hospital Eli had received medical care.

They did not know how many social workers there had been, and the one in question currently would change again, to a Looked After Child social worker.
Young people in these situations are known as LACS.
Some are known as 'lacs'.

Families at this stage, in residential placements, can share parental responsibility with the local authority. They have care orders in place. I did not have a care order. I had full parental responsibility for Eli.

Although the term 'parental responsibility' is a tenuous one.
The local authority does not behave like 'parents' although they are 'corporate' parents.

Bedtime stories, new shoes, visits to the seaside, picnics in the park, homework, pocket money, family 'in' jokes, cuddles and all-round love and care are not part of the responsibility they claim.

Reports and notes continued to be inaccurate, unfounded and started to become a little bit undone.
And meetings accrued and overlapped.

The initial COP hearing was on the same day as the first LAC review.

I could not be in both places at the same time.

But was nevertheless, I was held responsible for the one I did not turn up to.

Information about Eli and all about him made little sense.
Chronology of Eli was all over the place.

There were Looked After Child reviews every six months.
These gave the opportunity to all parties to give opinions.
Including me.

The reviewing officer kept changing.

One made the report review more about herself than the requirements of Eli.

The placement could not answer me when I asked whether Eli would go on the electoral role up there or at home.

They had never been braced with that question before.
Although the placement was full of young people eligible to vote.
Some of their young people were adults.

I was informed these young people were very vulnerable.
I emphasised even more reasons why they should be allowed to vote.
I put Eli on the electoral role here at home.

The social services had attempted to change the narrative to make it appear they had always been on board.
Supporting Eli.

The word 'support' is used frequently by all the principal services.
A word that appears in reports and other paperwork.

There is a difference between what is written and what is active.

In 2017, social services noted that Eli did not have mental health issues.
Yet it is reported in his EHCP that they supported us with his mental health issues.
To be clear, the social services were supporting my son with mental health issues they said he did not have.

The local authority wrote in their reports for the LAC reviews that I, had needed encouragement to get Eli into the hospital.

That I had to accept Eli needed medical help.

This had been coercively changed to make it appear that whilst the social services had been 'supporting' us they had also had to encourage me that Eli required medical help.

Whilst we had been screaming out for help.
And whilst they had provided nothing.

It was the professionals who had to accept Eli needed medical help.

I had needed no persuading my son required hospital.

It was changed in the reports.

After a few months of meetings, the independent reviewing officer would just copy and paste my remarks because they were too numerous, realistic, and honest, and could not be rewritten from a different perspective.

Basically, I was using my own narrative. Based on our own lived experiences.

The truth cannot be changed…no matter how hard one might try.

Outstanding

I had been informed that this placement was outstanding.

Therefore, I expected outstanding.

I expected masterful and exceptional, formidable, marvellous, impressive, and out of this world.

I also expected the promises made to Eli by the placement whilst he was in the third hospital, to be fulfilled.

This would be after the untimely commotion from the local authority.

I wanted outstanding, and nothing less would cajole me.

Thus, the fun and games commenced.

***

The placement staff's attitude towards us lacked compassion.

On visits, we were all monitored.

We were being observed.

As if in some way we were the cause for Eli being there.

There was some confusing detail about home life, but the general consensus now seemed to be about Eli being 'at risk' at home.

We had no idea how this idea had evolved.

Eli's mental health illness had been left far behind now.

When my sons enjoyed rough and tumble time, these were reported as incidents.

And had to be 'logged'.

Anything negative was logged.

The placement told me about his medication, including the methylphenidate he had taken all of his life for ADHD.

Eli did, however, come on many overnight home leaves, and each weekend. I made sure that physical contact was upheld and adhered to.

Medication was supposed to be counted out twice at the placement before Eli was driven home, however, on arrival, staff insisted on trudging through my house to a place where they could count through his medication. Otherwise, they could not release him into my care.

We were driven to our miserable lodgings on the outskirts of a motorway. A place we could not go anywhere with and were at the mercy of public transport. And the alternate weekends Eli came home.

During the first lockdown, in 2020, the local authority would not let Eli come home.
15 weeks without contact.
I was prevented from parenting my son and there were no contingency plans.
Whilst he could have come home, the local authority refused this to happen.

Legislation to take care of Eli, because of his time in the hospital, the DOLs, has stipulated to bring back to the attention of the court anything that restricted Eli at the placement.
His placement had become 'restricted' and the advocacy he was meant to receive did not exist.

I wrote to the MP and the Children's Commissioner.
And Eli's solicitor and his old patient advocate.
Everyone was adamant he should still be coming home.
The Law said he could come home.
The placement thought he should keep coming home, but the power in these decisions rested with the local authority.
They said he could not.
I took this back to the Court of Protection.

The Court of Protection was opened up again.

As regulations about the pandemic relaxed, Eli came home again.
And these leaves continued for the duration of the rest of his time at the placement.

His home leaves increased.
The LA SS and the placement could not find a reason why Eli should not spend more time at home.

He came on continued home leaves every weekend and all the holidays, because nobody could find a reason for him not to do this, additionally he was at home for several weeks at a time due to the COVID-19 outbreaks on site.

If I could not care for Eli, why was he being allowed to come home for weeks at a time?

He spent almost half the time in residential placement, at home.
Eli eventually REFUSED to go back.

He HATED the placement.

What was expected there and what I was promised, did not materialise.
Because there were so many outbreaks at the placement.
The safest place for Eli to be was at home.

Which threw the entire idea of me not being able to care for him out of the window.

It appeared more important for the placement to follow their routines and protocols, regardless of what was happening. Sometimes Eli was distressed, homesick and just wanted to talk.

***

The placement senior care worker had said my attitude had 'dropped off'.

She said I had to make Eli a priority, and Eli would need to be supervised around children and babies because it would create 'unspoken feelings'.

How she arrived at her information I had no idea.
And I do not know what an 'unspoken' feeling is.
She then left her position.

No one else at the placement was willing to discuss her views and some even said they did not know anything about it.

On one occasion on an overnight leave at home, we had all woken up late and therefore the schedule around Eli's medication was a bit late.

I was informed by the senior care worker that it was vital to medicate on time, to keep Eli focused.

Medication was messy, and undirected, when Eli was brought home to me.

Sometimes the staff could not remember when he was last medicated.

All in all, the "outstanding" behaviour that had been alluded by the LA and I had expected was less than satisfactory.

Eli was unhappy. His mental health was down played.

After less than 11 months in the placement after a particular incident there, Eli self-harmed.
This was because of a situation that had become out of hand.
In the classroom.

When Eli was confrontational to a member of staff at the placement, I was later informed by her that he was 'up in her face'.
The current local authority practice supervisor and her social worker at the time, who had never met Eli or me, said I was defensive and not truthful.
And needed to be more honest about things.

There was no particular reinforcement to these claims, other than they were not fully informed straight away about family changes at home.

The mental health care I had been promised for Eli that I had been told would be onsite at the placement was in fact in a town away from the placement.

Eli's mental health appeared to be an aftersight.

It is hard to keep people informed about changing circumstances at home when we do not know them, and they themselves keep changing.

Eli was meant to have an occupational therapist, a psychiatrist and a psychologist. He was meant to have a mental health advocate similar to the one in the hospital.

The locum psychiatrist had a few conversations with me.

She told me that the system was broken, and young people were falling through the cracks.

There was no onsite mental health for Eli, and any concerns at all would have to be taken up with local CAMHS back home.

So Eli came home.

I am unsure what was outstanding.

I was not the obstacle to things not being as they should have been.

I had gone along with everything.

Even at my displeasure.

And one day Eli refused to go back.

Part Five
Misconceptions and Meltdowns

"When will you get me out of here?"

—EKW

A CETR was organised when Eli stayed home.

This directed professionals around meaningful activities for Eli continued mental health care and resources for him to tap into for his exceptional needs.

The CETR is to keep Eli out of the hospital, so his requirements can be picked up in the community.

Lots of professionals turned up to this meeting. Everyone was logged and lots of promises were made.

Anything is possible if we stop relying on textbook formalities.

They do not contain the answer to all things.

Mechanical logic, surface value paperwork, two-dimensional paperwork.

Fresh air, innovation, new ideas, refreshes old ideas, and puts fresh energy into old beliefs. Blowing away the cobwebs from decomposing ideals that serve no further purpose and make no sense. This requires new thoughts and new people. Listening to our dependents.

Fresh air, innovation, new ideas, refreshes old ideas, and puts fresh energy into old beliefs.

Imagination and determination.

Things which may appear without solution can be resolved, with patience, time, clarity and, above all else, truth.

***

A provision was found for Eli that seemed to be able to meet his needs.

We were all aboard for this to happen until, last minute this provision U turned and rescinded their offer.

It was left to me to explain this to Eli.

***

The COP was still in process and mudslinging between the local authority and myself continued.

They made statements, and I responded to them.

The acting social worker was conveyed by the social services as nothing short of too good to be true.

Eli had some mental health psychology, which was touch and go.

After many months of nothing, another provision was found. A mainstream special needs unit for young people.

They were not given accurate information.

The social worker practice supervisor had accompanied Eli on his first meeting.

I had to wait outside because we were still amidst the bizarre rules of lockdown.
She was allowed to go through with Eli because she was social services.
I still have difficulty coming to terms with the protocols around social workers.
Including ones that just do not know us. At all.
Ones that do not know us, who have only recently come on board, and evident now more than ever, have little understanding of the past.

I remained outside.
With one of my daughters.
We watched as Eli had a total meltdown in the provision.
The social worker stood by watching him, helplessly.
She had no idea what to do.

I was kept outside.
The woman (me) who knew Eli better than anyone, and had to look on as her son, Eli, fell to the floor, in despair.
Flanked by provision staff and a social worker who had no idea how to cope with the situation.

One Ill-Prophesised Statement

"We have to make the change. Sometimes, it can only be us, so we have no choice but to get strong."

—EKW

One ill-prophesised statement and the child and the entire family are under threat.

If We Want Eli to Succeed

If Eli is given open choices, and it is left up to him to do whatever he wants, he will struggle.
He will probably choose a food outlet and go and eat somewhere.

If there is no clear structure, he will fall apart.

Trial and error mean some things will succeed whilst others will not. And it would be an individual choice of Eli how things would go.

Better to read those notes.

Mental Health

Mental health is a long, winding path into a labyrinth–vortex.
With convoluted arteries that become clogged, blocked and disconnected from the neural pathways. Creating all kinds of miscommunications that can affect mood, behaviours and all-round wellness.
The brain is so complex, so anything that emerges as an 'illness' can only be equally complex.

No one has the answers; no one knows quite what to do; we have to wait out the illness, keep watch, to make observations.

Nothing in mental health is particularly visible, or direct, or anything that makes much sense.

Not in the conventional way.
It is more about opening the box, kicking out the sides, coming away from the confines, and original concepts.

Mental health is a labyrinth.
It is not clean.
It is not comprehensible.

Once we have established this, the rest is pretty straightforward.

***

"It seems to me that the social worker is walking backwards through her life."
—EKW

We are told that we must cooperate with the social worker.

How do you cooperate with someone who is never around?

"It could be beneficial if the support workers around me could just do the same thing. It's simple really, so why can't they do that... I mean there are all these meetings... I don't know what anyone is talking about, do you?"

—EKW

The System

There is a uniform, single-pathway approach for young people who are involved in some way in the system.

The system should be influenced by its environment.
The system is a network of bureaucratic services and authorities with the active assistance of society.
Those that require parts of the system.

The system holds our information.

Information is then 'pulled' from the system.

The system is out of date.
The system is filled with people who do not take responsibility.

These people then argue with the family.
The parents.
The carers.
They argue with the truthtellers.

***

"Maybe they should all go back to school."

—EKW

People like Eli debunk myths about ASD and ADHD and certain sensory disorders, PDA and various mental health issues, and conditions and stuff about the mental health hospitals.

But it takes the rest of society and the professionals and all of the bureaucracy to listen.

It did not appear that the local professionals had much experience inside mental health hospitals.
Yet they seemed to have plenty to say about them.

And Eli.

And us.

"So we have a situation where we can become big, and get to the highest thing, but do they know what I am talking about."

—EKW

The CAMHS Psychiatrist

The post-hospital, local community CAMHS psychiatrist never met Eli.

His overview was that Eli had 'challenging behaviour' back in 2017 and that his diagnosis of schizoaffective disorder was a misdiagnosis.
How he arrived at this conclusion is unclear.

He had not met Eli, and CAMHS had been unsure why we wanted service from them again.

He wrote a letter to our GP containing his thoughts about misdiagnosis, he also wrote a synopsis of how he believed things had gone.

Dates, events and timelines in his letter were in such confusion that it was appalling.
He included an unmethodical, disarranged series of events, which made no sense.
I challenged his letter and his opinion and wrote to the GP and complained about my concerns.
I took my concern to CAMHS complaints, and they upheld it.

The worry is that a consultant psychiatrist's opinion can carry weight.

The Adult Mental Health
Services Psychiatrist

In adult services, the adult consultant psychiatrist upheld the diagnosis of Schizo affective disorder, stating it was correct and medication effective, for the time when Eli had become unwell.

And for what he had experienced.

CAMHS Intervention Crisis

A great deal of intense psychiatric disorders can begin to develop in the early teens.

Suspicion, anxiety, disordered thinking, immense fear, overwhelming worry, post-traumatic stress and illogical behaviours…overlapping already existing ASD and ADHD diagnoses can create some chaos in the mind.
There is little etiquette in any illness.
Their body has broken down.
The mind is confused.
The concept of psychosis is a labyrinth.
When little makes sense, it can lead to a total breakdown.

The crisis team is apparently a team of mental health professionals around Eli able to interact with his behavioural difficulties and bring him to a place of recovery.
Restoring his mental health well-being or making moves to assess him.
Calling the crisis team should warrant that the person is now reaching out for further assistance. Because they are in crisis.

He was displaying critical symptoms. He was unhinged, and shouting because he was afraid. He was hallucinating and paranoid. These were attributes of his Psychosis.
Nevertheless, the crisis team hung up on him.
He had upset them.
They didn't like people shouting at them. They didn't tolerate abuse.
I am still unsure how we should behave when Eli is in Crisis.
In that we do not distress the CRISIS team.

Has Anything Been Established

What has been established by now is that the authorities resented me.
I challenged them.
Called them out on things they had promised.
They could not tell me what to do, and I called out their failures.
I repeated back to them, their words.

The opposite of love is indifference.
So, if hate exists, we are still in with a chance.
Passion elicits all kinds of emotions.

They hated me.

They are not who they boast to be.
They do not fulfil their pledges.
There is no point saying you will commit to something you have no intent of honouring.
The only qualification that has any value in life is in the education of a human being's behaviour. Their conduct towards another human being. To value the person in front of us.

I do not get angry.
If I am angry, I can be controlled.
And someone needs to be worth my anger.
It is not a usual emotional response from me.
And uses valuable energy.

For the failures we faced constantly, and, their lack of cooperation, they turned it onto me; saying that I refused to cooperate.

What upset me and irritated me before, things that had been inferred and directly criticised about me, no longer had bearing.

For these unkind things to be said, I would first have to value the opinion.

I brought many issues to the wide-open table of this relationship.
And told the truth.

It was much like a disintegrating marriage where one partner is putting in too much.

When cohorts were summoned and assembled for annual reviews, this was when battle commenced.

Without much left to use as evidence, because the chips are down, they have done no work and have not turned up or attempted contact, they turn this onto me and smear my character and reputation.

It is now written that I refused to cooperate with authorities.
It does not take long for someone to believe their own lies.
By the time a new worker is joined, they just read whatever fabricated notes have been passed along.
It is all somewhat predictable and yet they seem to get away with it.
Senior leads in meetings and, even my own lawyers, tell me I really need to start working with the local authority.
Regardless of the copious attempts to do just that.

Having not known my family or anything about us, our background and culture, just plain and simply unable to speak of us as if they knew us, the odds were stacked up against us. Still no mention of mental health intervention. It has become a social service issue.
I was still being told that I really needed to work with the local authority, and cooperate.
How do we cooperate with un cooperative people?

Still we (families and carers) were at fault. It was never far from my mind the insurgence of utter chaos. The world we had once relied upon, to provide medicine for the poison that had infected all of us

And this is something deeply rooted in the system that has to be tackled.

If we refuse to acknowledge any failures we cannot improve. The fight for justice is a cruel, twisted path.

The fundamental purpose to any of us on Earth is our behaviour as human beings to one another.

It is difficult to become bulletproof:
To come back untouched and unscathed.
I have come to realise I am dealing with people who cannot see me if I leave their eyeline.
Once out of view, I no longer exist.

***

I became aware that I was still hoping and waiting for something that was never going to happen.

Fight Down the Proud

Those who strive in the face of hardship are magnificent. True soul hard workers.
Guardians of the homelands, champions to our children.
Frontliners.
Not ever letting down the guard.
Closing ranks; summoning up strength to defeat the self-regarding pompous attitudes of those we had turned to.
For help.
Comfort, reassurance.
We put our faith and trust in local services, because we have to.

The CAMHS Psychologist

Eli had psychologist appointments every week.

Sometimes, he took off his shoes and T-shirt, which are indicators that he has some issues to resolve.

He might stand on the table.

What would become the last CAMHS psychology appointment was the finale of everything.

Eli had woken bright and happy, we walked to the appointment. We talked about his new phone and earphones that would accompany them.

He hugged me in the waiting room, and then his psychologist appeared and his face changed.

Hours went by, whilst I listened to the sounds of my son crying out, shouting, screaming and yelling.

At one point, I demanded to know what was going on and saw the state of my son.

He had dishevelled the poky little room he was in, he only wore his trousers, his hair was hanging in his face and his eyes were glazed.

The former illness had returned.

The one that apparently did not exist.

In a matter of approximately 20 minutes, my son had transformed from a bright, happy, enthusiastic young man into a psychotically out-of-control, disturbed person.

He screamed at me to leave him alone, to get out of his life, he swore and said he did not feel safe.

Know your subject.
Know the words they use. Why do they use them?
Know he is past being well.
He has become totally out of control.
What he says makes no sense.

It is usual to not want the family home, the safety, the security.
They say terrible things, we have all learned to rise above, move beyond them and deal with the situation at hand.
I thought CAMHS would do this.

But they didn't.
They panicked!

Insanity Returned

The rages of the worst hell were let loose and worst still when those meant to be helping had no idea what to do.

They have not listened; they have not familiarised themselves with his notes.

Eli self-harmed in her session.

Several times.

The psychologist came out of the session to ask for details about the social worker.

The psychologist was also known as the care coordinator.

She had no idea of Eli's medication.

I had thought that the local CAMHS were the community extension of the mental health hospitals.

Eli continued to cry out and pull apart the room he was confined to.

The psychologist came out again to tell me Eli was having an 'outburst' and they were going to take Eli to the local district hospital.

She also told me they were going to walk to the hospital.

Eli could be heard all over the clinic.

He was shouting, screaming, spitting, foaming...

He had become dishevelled and enraged.

No other staff members went into the room, and Eli was not encouraged.

The hospital was approximately 40 minutes away by foot.

My son was now deranged and out of control.

He had not eaten since breakfast and had not stepped outside the little room in hours.

I felt a vexed moment of relapse, as I remembered back to 2017, September 14. 10 hours in the CAMHS hub with nothing to show for it and no follow-up care.

Eli was at his highest point of vexation.

Staggeringly, I had helped co-write reports and points, in a step-by-step procedure, of how Eli could be managed should he begin to exhibit signals of distress, disorientation and at worst psychosis, to prevent him from becoming unmanageable.
These notes were unknown and unheeded.

Walking anywhere outside in the open at this point would put my son, themselves and anyone else at huge risk.
This was a high-risk alert.
Eli was not calm.
He could not make much sense of the world around him.
He was hungry and thirsty, deluded and volatile, something had triggered him.
Whatever had triggered him had been in the room with the psychologist.

I was concerned that walking for 40 minutes in the community with professionals who did not know him and had little idea what to do, would set Eli at a great disadvantage.

The psychologist made an excuse about not being able to take him in her car.
I was shocked by everything.

The social worker called me and told me to go home.
There was no way I was leaving my son in the incapable hands of anyone right now.
And it would be disregarding the DOL order.
And I could not trust anyone to not just call the police.
I ordered and paid for a taxi, and once at the hospital, Eli ran through the corridors telling everyone to have me arrested.

I sat outside the hospital.

The psychologist came out to me and asked if I would come in and tell the A&E staff about Eli's prescribed medication.

She also said she didn't want another 'outburst'.

She referred to Eli's autism-related and ADHD-related meltdown, a breakdown of sensory overload as an 'outburst'.

She is a mental health professional, and she has described my son's meltdown as an 'outburst'.

I went into the A&E examination room, told them what they needed to know and left some snacks and a drink for Eli on the radiator for him, as he was still snarling at me, and I took a quick note of the information the hospital staff had for me.

I had to smile, as the personal details, contacts, etc were incorrect and not up to date.

I began to consider now that out-of-date information across the board, on The System, was just a thing now.

Ignorance versus stupidity?

Eventually, Eli came out of the hospital with the psychologist, he was calmer and ready to go home.

I called a taxi and told the psychologist she could walk.

Once home Eli was fine.

He reverted to his old ways, filled with remorse and could not do enough to help me and say sorry.

He vacuumed his room, took a bath, ate a hearty dinner, and explained later in the evening that he was simply fed up and frustrated by the lack of action around him.

And that professionals did not know what to do, or enough about him.

Tellingly this behaviour is triggered by the lack of professional input and knowledge about Eli.

A young man who has experienced a breakdown emotionally, who has been in hospital for almost two years, and residential placement for almost a year.

Back in the community things were as they had always been, once before. We were thrown into the deep end of rhetoric and words and dialogue.

Textbook dialogue, vague responses to my questions.
A system that is supposed to look after the neediest and the most vulnerable. I was yet to see this in action.
The vulnerable get left behind.

The Response

I demanded a full explanation from the psychologist.

I had an idea of what to expect, and I knew she would not take responsibility. I had a feeling I would be patronised, and the situation down played, with whatever negatives thrown over to the family.

When pushed, the psychologist responded. I knew she did not want to communicate with me.

But there was enough legislation around Eli. And he wanted an explanation.

The legislation protected his rights at least.

She explained that Eli had arrived at her clinic already in a state of distress and loaded the blame entirely onto the family.

She went on to explain that her 'team' did not think the diagnosis of Schizo affective disorder was 'helpful' for Eli.

She gave some insipid explanations about understanding how I felt.

I explained to her that and none of her selections of adjectives came anywhere close to how I felt.

The psychologist explained in her reply that Eli's feelings ran away with him.

She inferred no accountability at all.

She did remind me she was 'highly specialised'.

I told her in response that her use of words to purportedly reflect my feelings and what my feelings were did not do justice to Eli, or his conditions, and had not implemented her better judgement.

In my opinion, my son became triggered whilst in the session, and this can be overbearing. Maybe she panicked.

I also asked her to stop analysing me.

We were immensely let down.
For her failures, and refusal to acknowledge them, the entire day in the CAMHS collapsed. Again.

After the stockpiles of notes over the years about Eli, assessments and reports, and so on, it is detailed that if anyone is going out with my son, they should have all his details.

They should always go to the hospital prepared.
Water, provisions, drinks, food, bandages, emergency medication and a change of clothes.

Quick thinking.
A carer's thinking.
A kind person's thinking.

Had my son been catered for correctly and his 'outburst' been looked after in the right way he would not have gouged open a past and very old self-harm wound. Then there would have been no need for A&E.

It is a very sad state of affairs to have to tell the mental health services how to behave when my son has become unhinged.

The fact they were trying to reason with him, was a total waste of time.
In the declining state, he was in.
Disregarding everything he has been through and everything any of the other more proficient professionals around him have achieved.

At the point someone has become mentally unwell, different protocols need to take place.

A different direction.

The autism brain reacts and processes information differently.

The ADHD brain processes information at a different cognitive level than non-ADHD.

The psychotic mind when overloaded will become completely delusional.

3 major conditions.

Each has a spectrum of unlimited symptoms and characteristics.

And each personal to that person.

***

Eli does not have 'outbursts'.

Autism does not have 'outbursts'.

The commentary from the psychologist trivialised Eli's meltdown.

A serious sensory situation.

It indicated that the professionals did not have a strong enough concept about Eli's autism and disregarded his ADHD.

During Eli's life, I have been informed we all have a bit of autism in us. There is no such thing as a "bit of autism".

And there is no linear perspective. Autism is a spectrum. Without beginning or end, without mild to severe. Autism is existing and it is preferred to use Autism Spectrum Disorder. In this way everyone with Autism has their place and their right to the condition.

My son was overloaded in her session and something triggered him. He also had psychosis, "sleeping" in the background of his mental state.

Nothing was going to help Eli that day.

Apart from the change of scenery.

And a re-direction of focus, and of words.

That did not happen, resulting in him falling apart, and deteriorating rapidly.

The psychologist ended her commentaries by saying she would make another appointment.

But she never did.

She did not follow up with a call or anything else.

She never spoke to Eli again.

This became her last session with my son and it was still two months before he became an adult.

She wrote Eli a letter of goodbye with animations and pictures.

All things that can trigger Eli.

It's all in the notes.

He needs help to understand the basic format of things.

Eli does not read or comprehend very well a lot of words, or letters.

He did not understand it.

He kept asking when his new appointment with her would be.

She told me to take up things with adult services, and we never saw her again.

She abandoned Eli.

Notes...and Paperwork

"Do any of these people even know me."

—EKW

What happens to the notes?

Legal statements, police reports, third-party opinions, points of view, services, care teams and independent professionals, including my own work.
Events, things of importance, evidence for study, bullet points.

Countless, multifarious, interminable documented emails and chronologies, and other writings over the years, co-written with workers, applications, my personal viewpoints and so on.
Amassed from Child in Need meetings, Team around the Child meetings, risk assessments, positive behaviour reports, excessive notes written by social workers, and other arbitrary notes put together by local community CAMHS.

CETR, Care Programme Approaches and Multidisciplinary Meetings, psychiatric points of view; from those who have known Eli well and those who have no idea who he is.
Court of Protection hearings, tribunal cases.

Notes are passed along from one set of professionals to the next, predecessor to successor.
Information is moved and lost, rewritten or missed out altogether.
Everything is messy and out of context.
Chronology is chaotic, and the background of Eli bears little resemblance to how things were.

Rather like a game of Chinese whispers.

We can never be quite sure what we will end up with.

Eli is left at a loose end and a disadvantage.

Because no one knows who Eli is?

***

Dialogue can change perspectives and change opinions.
It can transform attitudes.
Refresh perspectives.
Dialogue is only effective when all sides are willing to listen.

And dialogue opens up a way through difficult, complex situations. We simply cannot lose sight of what is important, of our dreams and aspirations, or the fight for justice.

Eli

"There is a purpose to me you know."

—EKW

In some cases, Eli can make very capable decisions and has done so, sometimes in very trepid and volatile situations.

Eli can be forgetful, and confuse things that he wants. He has little concept of time or money and admits himself he requires assistance always.
Sometimes, he is just not in the right frame of mind.

Eli frequently has conversations with entities in his head. He tells me they are not people or voices but higher beings.
They are benign and offer comfort to him.

There is a great deal of trial and error.
Things do not always run smoothly, and we worry about everything, all the time.
We worry about the future; we worry about what will happen to Eli when I am gone.
We worry about when he gets old.
His focus and attention are extremely limited.
Eli becomes irritated and confused by the professionals and the system.
He is always very direct with his workers about what he wants to happen.
He has always been extremely direct with everyone.
Including me.

Eli has a million dreams.

It is a continual challenge to be Eli, every day.

Eli's Home: It is All in the Notes

"Have they read about me yet?"

—EKW

When Eli refused to go back to the residential placement he arrived once more to the community care of social services and the mental health teams.

It was a strange sort of dark repetition of a few years before, back to the time before the hospital.
We returned to nothing.

Nothing was in place for him.

***

Strong Legislation surrounded Eli.
Examples are Section 117 and a DOLs order in place by the Court of Protection.
These were there to protect his requirements, and his way of life.
And because he had been in a mental health hospital under section.

***

Nothing was prepared and put into place to settle him into community life, and we struggled.
All of us in my family.
Once more.

It seemed the conversations once had whilst in residential placement with social workers about Eli returning home for good, and what he would do, disappeared into the ether.

The social workers continued to change.

It is not possible to form a relationship with anyone if they keep changing or are never around.

What had been enthusiastically promised for Eli in the community, in meetings and at court hearings by services did not materialise.

The copious and laborious meetings across the years, at home, in the community, at the hospital the residential placement at court and so on, the accumulated notes about Eli from all directions and from all professional pathways piled up, and gathered dust.

They were unread.

I was told "basic information" was provided for bodies of people who said they could meet Eli's needs.

For someone as complex as Eli and with his background and tumultuous history, basic was just not good enough.

It sets both Eli and future workers up to fail.

The failure to deliver what was supposed to be in place for Eli was blamed upon me.

The local authority social care services were demoralising and reproachful toward me and cast unnecessary aspersions.

They broadcast the worst areas of our lives, and the smallest parts of the year where untimely dire incidents had happened with Eli, and whispered inaudibly his successes for the rest of the year.

They were too concerned with themselves and their own accolades yet kept tripping up over their own shortcomings.

The DOLs was late for renewal. I insisted it was renewed.

The thing is if it was let go, then my son would have nothing.

And if he became unwell once more, we would be in the same difficulties as we had already experienced before.

In 2017.

The worries that the local authority had once had, during County Court, were short-lived and seemed only appropriate in those few moments.

Because these worries no longer existed.

***

Mental Health hospital far outweighed the residential placement, yet the latter was where all the emphasis lay.

The local authority derailed the original series of events around Eli, in that he had experienced a vast mental health emotional breakdown, which was later upheld and diagnosed as schizoaffective disorder; instead, the local authority services made it about him having learning disabilities.

Unfortunately, this pigeonholed Eli.

And created some upheaval in the mental health service community.

***

The local CAMHS mental health services in the community had no idea why we wanted continued care for him.

This surprised me considering the length of time he had been in the hospital.

Under the Mental Health Act.

On section.

And why they did not know.

***

So the promised life skills and the promises from the actual placement were not delivered.

I chased the mental health team for 16 months, during which the adult psychologist gave a variety of reasons why she could not see him, principally that Eli was expected to rearrange his timetable around her availability.

She made no effort to meet Eli.

To check on him.

She did communicate with me many times. It appears that from these conversations, she devised a crisis plan.

She used information from an old chronology I had put together from some years before.

It read like a tabloid newspaper. Bits of our lives contorted, out of context like canards of sensational news.

Although Eli now had been known to the mental health services since 2017, it took many months and a severe complaint to mental health services, for some rudimentary involvement to be put in place.

The adult psychiatrist upheld the mental health diagnosis of schizoaffective disorder and continued to check Eli's medication.

I had expected the mental health services and crisis involvement to have information and understanding of who Eli is and what is required.

This was not the case.

They also appeared unable to know what to do, or how to treat him.
They were unaware of his history.

I had been hopeful that common sense might have prevailed; that the assistance of local care services at home would follow on from the hospital.

***

We discovered Eli should have had a mental health social worker.
This was apparently written into documents from years ago.
It was understandable I was becoming immensely frustrated by the lack of information and coordination from the principal services.

I was also very surprised at the lengths services would take, elaborating about things they never gave us in the first place. Friends, family, neighbours offered their support. Sometimes just being around us, helped. But it was their experiences, of having been through what we were going through, that assisted us the most. Whilst the services sat still.

The adult social services had to be prompted into almost everything expected of them.

They had given Eli the option of how much he wanted them to be involved in his life, and he chose very little.

They seemed to accept this.

However, it did not stop them from turning up to an activity a few months later. Unannounced, and uninvited.

This threw Eli and his key worker, and his guard was pulled up immediately.

He was placed at a disadvantage. Both he and I were unprepared.

This put Eli very ill at ease and on guard.

He had no idea what was happening and neither did his key worker on the activity.

However, a quick snap judgement about Eli's frame of mind and mental health well-being were able to be made by the acting social worker in just a few minutes.

They told me they had been unable to call me about turning up beforehand.

They told me this when they called me straight after.

Therefore, everything recorded in the notes that kept amassing about Eli was ignored.

How to approach things, what language to use and so on, was unused.

But it's all there, in the notes.

***

A mainstream provision was found for Eli.

He had never been educated in mainstream and was expected to sit all day in a mainstream class.

This was all the local authority had been able to find.

Eli had become distressed at not being able to call me in this setting and had become volatile.

He kicked and threw things around.

The provision's response was to lock him out of their setting.

And leave him in the community, alone.

Eli was terrified.

He was in the middle of a busy main road. People he did not know were all around him. He was locked out of the provision that was meant to keep him safe. He began to cry and ran up to some strangers to ask if they could help him and give him a hug.

It was a member of the public that kept Eli safe and looked after him.

Someone totally unknown to us. It was a couple with a baby, who took Eli in their arms and held him, looked at his lanyard, and saw my number. They immediately called me and sat with him close by the education provision, until I managed to arrive in a taxi. They were shocked he had been left alone, and I have no idea what might have happened otherwise. Had it not been for them, my son would have been at considerable risk. Alone, unsupervised. Eli cannot fend for himself independently. He requires supervision all the time. Effectively, the provision that had said they could meet his needs, could not.

A member of the public who did not know him, could.

Instructions everywhere on orders and plans stipulate that Eli requires continued support and assistance.

And must not be left on his own.

He would become too distressed and would not make coherent choices.

His forgetfulness, lack of attention and ability to focus in the moment could put him at very high risk.

His conditions are written about and explained in detail.

There is response literature about how to cope with Eli in particular settings, or where he might become upset, and behave irrationally.

Taking steps to reduce his anxieties and any volatile, abusive, violent, unhinged behaviours.

However, these can happen and can be unpredictable.

Yet for all the legislation, notes, reports and accrued paperwork about Eli, it appears if Eli exhibits any of these characteristics, he is then held for ransom.

He is condemned for the very traits his conditions exhibited.

Things without purpose, and open choices, render Eli bored, resistant and possibly at the mercy of his own conditions.

The organisations who say they can meet his needs along with the services that provide the information become a juxtaposition: if both sides do not properly communicate and do not have the correct information in the first place, Eli suffers.

Workers from other organisations have ended up in tears, shaken and behaved irrationally.

Not knowing how best to deal with Eli, because inadequate information was given about him.

In the first place.

Professionals still went ahead and contacted me, using numbers that were on the 'system' but had been obsolete or just did not exist.

People came to meetings we did not know.

They were all referred to by name.

I was referred to as 'Mum'.

Boiling Frogs

During the course of things, we, like Eli, became quickly adaptive to our emotional surroundings.

We were a family swimming about at room temperature.

Never quite knowing when the heat would arrive underneath us.

This kind of sensory adaptation was a sort of gradual thing, over the years. Never quite knowing what would happen next from those services, so desperately out of touch, and not interested, yet on paper appearing as if they were with us every step of the way.

We never got used to the unpredictability of how things might occur; we just became accustomed to some shocking situations we were put in.

***

The social care services complained I used emails to communicate and that I had held the social worker at arm's length, preventing her from working with Eli.

They told me I had been challenging mental health services and was rude, offensive and often disparaging to social care service workers.

Averting your gaze from the actual situation creates future chaos.

Accusing parents of not doing things without any evidence to support, is a waste of time.

I would say categorically that the system used to invoke care services and other local authority areas of society, everything that is contained within the system, is a huge disappointment of democratic living and welfare.

The vigilant do not die

Those who neglect are as if dead.

Pointing a finger at me suggesting I am the crux of the problem is a lost cause. When correct information is not given, it can set people like my son up to fail.

Autism was never an issue. Eli had never been diagnosed with Learning Disabilities.
The major challenges lay in Eli's mental health.
Schizoaffective Disorder.
A parent who is calling out for help; is someone who needs help.
With vulnerable people we must always be on guard around them. Aware of the details, the information, and what should be accomplished.
If notes have been written and accumulated then these must be read.

I had expected at the very least, some human empathy and a basic level of compassion and sympathy.

Activities

What has worked for Eli has been the selfless efforts made by third parties, and by members of my family, putting things in place to attempt to help Eli become more productive in society.

These people have taken account of the dreams and desires of Eli and his future ambitions and have also taken on board the bizarre, delusional and sometimes impossible wishes of Eli.

What matters is that Eli is heard and understood; that he is given hope and that possibility can exist in the dark corners of his life.

That being Eli is a massive challenge every day for him.

And what darkness can shroud areas of society should not cloud the possibilities of anyone if their imaginations are large enough.

Activities and the people that have been successful with Eli have worked beyond their own payrolls.

Determined to get things right for him.

They may not always be fully aware of autism, or ADHD or Psychosis, but what matters to them, is Eli.

What Eli wants and how to make him happy.

Eli's self-confidence rockets and his belief in society is restored.

It encourages Eli to take giant leaps of faith he might never have considered before.

With time, effort and patience.

This has been my son's experiences since his decline, since the hospital and since the residential school and back in the community.

A faithful narrative.

They Did Not See What We Saw

"They should just tear everything down into pieces and start all over again."

—EKW

A person, who can, no matter how desperate the situation, give another person hope has the qualities of a true leader.

There is always room for improvement.

My son's breakdown in 2017 and the surprising and unfolding events that followed over the years opened my eyes.

What I had expected from the local shared assigned care services did not materialise.
I was able to first-hand experience the utter turmoil of the care and social services, and others also affiliated.
No one communicated with one another.
Through my long, unconventional life anyhow, I have observed those who get by using cunning and lies, deceit, vague responses and rhetorical replies.

People who do not respond directly, honestly, and humanely challenge the trust of those who do.
Those with integrity.
I was held responsible by the authorities who said I held workers at arm's length, and prevented them from working with Eli.

I was informed I was disparaging, and was the reason for so many vacillating workers.
In my opinion. blaming anyone for what has not been provided, and for any shortcomings, is the real failure.

From my perspective, protocol took precedence over the person.

Eli became unwell in early 2024. It happened again.
Eli's medication had been reduced until it stopped.
Then he mentally collapsed.
This produced terror of heart for my family. Knowing the past. Knowing the traumas.
Then Eli mentally collapsed.
Once more darkness arrived in his life. And dripped over into ours.
His paranoia terrified him, and he hallucinated badly.
His psychiatrist re medicated him immediately and we managed to keep Eli from hospital.
He was moved from Learning disabilities to community Mental Health.

Eli has learned to live with the hallucinations that visit him. And he has understood that the insouciance of services around him are not my fault. His world can be cold and dark.
Violence has left him these days, delusion and paranoia have not.
Eli is a strong young man, admirable in his challenges, and he is fully aware about how things really are. His illness hangs about in the background, in ambush, ready to launch. We will never be prepared, but at least we will be there for him.

I confess I worry all the time if another relapse happens, or if he crumbles completely.

Insanity is not just reserved for those who struggle mentally. Chaos exists in the world around us.
People are not always who we think they are.
Those with responsibility for the welfare of our vulnerable, do not fulfil the task.
Consequently, my son has shifted from pillar to post.

***

Part Six
Food For Thought

"You know there is a higher purpose."

—EKW

My son Eli will arrive at his own conclusions about things in his own way.
Eli leaves an indelible trace of himself on people everywhere.
This is because he is extraordinary.
Yet he has been in the hands of some pretty ordinary professionals.

The only disability lies within society.
These are the mindsets of authorities meant to be keeping us all safe.
Vulnerable people are not disabled.

In conclusion, if the principal services could not handle my son, Eli, at his most crumpled then they did not deserve to be a part of him at his best.

We cannot underestimate our enemy.
Especially when we believed them to be our friends.
This is difficult because we have to be prepared for things we do not know will happen. And we do not understand them.
Yet we have to work with them.
So we keep them close and observe them.
And we close ranks and use the battle cry. For victory and voices to be heard, and solidarity amongst others, and for possibility.

The local community services were supposed to be available for Eli.

Eli became very unwell, mentally unwell, in 2017 and the cohort services meant to be at his service were not.

They ignored him.

Whilst this is totally unacceptable, I could have let it go, what stopped me was; When Eli finally went into the hospital on section, the local services pretended they had cared.

They pretended they had been involved.

That hurt.

Consequently, these erroneous actions have caused untold problems moving forward.

Unwarranted action has been taken, and we have all been moved in a variety of directions, none of which make much sense from where this all began.

Being unable to take responsible for the truth, has created travesty upon parody, resulting in something that bears little resemblance to what we started out with.

The Local Authority Social Services are not disturbed by Eli's situation or his conditions, they are temporarily disturbed by the current circumstances.

Because I challenged them and became the anomaly. I also challenged the mental health services.

I strongly when believe people constantly tell you about their qualities; they don't have them.

People who possess such distinguished positive qualities, do not have to broadcast them.

We have never received any counsel, nor have we received respite or relief. We have received little understanding and very limited empathy, and I have yet to feel the tenderness of sympathy. We have received however more than enough criticism and reproach.

The local services started off on the wrong foot and have turned around in circles ever since.

Services for all that they have agreed and promised, have delivered very little.

Titles, years of academic training, theory, academic prowess and qualifications do not qualify anyone; education is conveyed in our behaviour. How a person conducts themselves towards others. Throughout society.
Whoever we are.

It is interesting to learn things about yourselves that never happened, from people that do not know you.
And how much a body of services will attempt to elaborate on something they never gave us in the first place.

I have been argued with, condemned, reproached, talked over and ignored over the years.
I have seen words I have said and written, used out of context, and the shortcomings of the professional services bounced back to me.
They have used my information and made it their own.
There have been a great many holes in the fabric of Eli's history, written by the principal services, and many blank spaces and there still are, because the services had not been involved and had simply not taken him, or our original cries for help, seriously.
Reports I have read, from the cohort of care services, have stumped me to varying degrees because the content has not matched the reality.

Furthermore, they have been written by people who have either never met us or know very little about us.
Poor information can create more damage than good.

I should never have to argue or fight for basic humanistic empathy.

Those people who have helped us have been on the same journey.
They are the monarchs of the streets.
They are the open wilderness of society.
Kings and queens of the community hold up the framework for other families.

They are the autism families, mental health families and ADHD families.
They are all the neurodivergence, the vulnerable, the needy and the ignored.

These are not professional care services; they are everyday ordinary citizens who came to our rescue.

Those who have battled on, with their own dependents.
Through the quagmire of bureaucracy and non-attentive care services.
They know the way and illuminate the way enough for others, and we all stumble through.
They threw the rope into the hole we fell into and pulled us out.
These are the worthies and the sages, the wise and compassionate, the knowledgeable and the benevolent; they are the general public, people of our streets, the carers, and other disabled vulnerable wise ones, who have helped me hold my family together.

They have kept us moving and gave us hope.
When no one else did.
They listened and offered support when no one else did.

They are the real people, the survivors, the ones like us who have travelled the arduous trek through bureaucratic decisions, and care orders, and outlandishly deep piles of paperwork; notes and reports and assessments that sit and gather dust.

They are also aggrieved and mishandled.
Allowing us to lean upon them until we were able to find our own way home.

We are part of the fabric of the community.
We do this out of love and commitment to our dependents, the ones we love.
We fight the system, and we fight another system that pays us.
And takes money from us when we did not expect it.
I still hold out hope that services considered to be the tenets of society will actually aid those who are buckling under the pressure.
If there are adjustments, changes, less than expected money. I realise now it is all a sort of an element of surprise.

I must make arduous, laborious phone calls, and wait in ultra lengthy queues, whilst caring for my son and taking care of all the other necessary things in daily life.

And continue to fight the system, that is too burdened by paperwork to care.

A system that is stretched and worked to its limits.

A system that holds me responsible for the ongoing issues with Eli, in his daily life.

None of us are perpetrators, we are all struggling to one extent or another, but only some of us admit this.

This can change in a moment if everyone could admit their foibles, admit mistakes, and learn from them.

We are still amidst exploring unknown frontiers, those services we had hoped would be our friends have no intention of befriending us.

The simplified cut and dry approach they desire to use for everyone just cannot work with nexus of conditions and symptoms of someone like my son.

I cannot trust the local services because they have little confidence in themselves. They keep changing focus.

Every time they select something to focus on, it does not stay in place, because what they have chosen is just a small component of a much larger, labyrinthal, multiplex of focuses with my son.

It is not straight forward, and neither will it ever be.

It is a sad but brutal reality that things must become so bad, and so awful, before professionals meant to be looking after vulnerable people, get involved.

We cannot invent the truth.

It must be recalled.

There is magic in Eli's meltdowns, and we can turn his pain into passion, by turning all this poison into medicine.

Anything can be transformed, no matter how impossible, how dismal, how difficult, how mixed up.

There is always a solution.

We must have faith. And the ability to converse.

And listen.

Without dialogue, we remain ignorant.

Without dialogue, we cannot learn, and there is always something to learn.

We learn by obstacles; we learn by mistakes; our attitude to how we make future decisions is based upon these obstacles and defines the future.

Creating value inside the darkness.

Conclusion

We gave the canons of our communities across our country too much rope, and they swung us from their own pitiful gallows.

One ill-prophesised statement and the child and the entire family are under threat.
And the establishment offers little emotional respite.
To find out where we are now, we really need to take a good look at the past.
We are only here because of what happened back then.

I had looked to professionals to uphold the precepts of those troubled, vulnerable, and in need.
I have been greatly dissatisfied.

In the very beginning, we were not believed, and Eli's breakdown was not taken seriously.
He became worse, and we struggled.
In the beginning, principal services ignored the emergency and downplayed the issues.
They dismissed the actual challenges we had and later on during the course of all things, broadcast our worst moments, the direst of situations, and they spoke barely to a whisper of the truth.

It could have broken us, were it not for our own volition and conviction of faith.
We had to believe that help would come at some point.

I also came to understand that anyone living in an unorthodox way; anything eccentric, unusual and beyond what might be considered normal social mainstream, was just a nuisance to the local authorities and mental health services.

Then I came to understand that being outspoken and challenging the way of things was equally bothersome to them.

When we want change, we need everything around us to change.

We have to know the change we want.

That is a hard task, difficult, sometimes, impossible.

This is what I have tried to do.

I have not given up and continue to keep challenging the system.

I do not take the bait. I do not get angry. I take on the upsurge with different ammunition.

I use the truth.

"You see we must get to the higher place.

Everything you can think of, the biggest thing that ever you can think of like a whole army...they are inside my head, and they are just like...there. They give me headaches, I would like to talk to some kind of doctor to see what it is and maybe even take it away.

Or not take it away, because it's my head, and they belong to me I suppose, but to see what it is.

And just let people know what is going on.

Is there stuff in other people's heads? Voices?

And just, things. It's made out of gods and wishes and magic.

And planets, it goes further than all the planets, and all the universes, it's so big, bigger than the biggest thing, on the highest level.

And when I can get there, and make it smaller then everything will be in place."

—EKW

The System Must Change

"If you want to know me you have to get inside my head, and then you have to become really small to do that."

—EKW

The chapters turn pages when we can use any kind of regret and suffering and transform it into jewels of something possible.

Aggressiveness is never met with joy.
Inciting fear cannot be harnessed with friendship.
Families need hope, we all need hope.
We continue with the battle cry.
Because we have to.
For those that cannot fight back and cannot speak up.
For the vulnerable, and impeded, for our disabled, neurodivergent and mentally challenged.
For all the reasons that we are carers.

Monsters are created by their own relentless unforgivable actions; the most beautiful are found inside the souls with no ego.

We can only become what we want through our own transformation.
Only through our emancipation will we lead others to victory.
And a true leader inspires others, selflessly, and sets direction for everyone, they communicate, motivate, and deliver.
They know when to stand down.

Hope creates possibility and can unleash unparalleled potential.

Until then we must remain undefeated, unwavering in our conviction and keep chipping away for change.

Take care of what needs to be done. Legal does not equal justice. Justice is what we fight for. For victory, balance, accord, for happiness and fairness and a voice. The system has to change.

Dreams and Hopes and Keeping the World Alive

With thanks and deep humility to all my children.

All of you are totally off the grid and you really worked me.

I was born from the unconventional. So were you.

And I would never have done any of it without any of you by my side.

The End

www.ingramcontent.com/pod-product-compliance
Lightning Source LLC
Chambersburg PA
CBHW060458290526
45791CB00001B/166